Words Underway

Words Underway

Continental Philosophy of Language

Carolyn Culbertson

ROWMAN & LITTLEFIELD
INTERNATIONAL

London • New York

Published by Rowman & Littlefield International, Ltd.
6 Tinworth Street, London SE11 5AL
www.rowmaninternational.com

Rowman & Littlefield International, Ltd. is an affiliate of
Rowman & Littlefield
4501 Forbes Boulevard, Suite 200, Lanham, Maryland 20706, USA
With additional offices in Boulder, New York, Toronto (Canada), and London (UK)
www.rowman.com

British Library Cataloguing in Publication Information
A catalogue record for this book is available from the British Library

ISBN: HB 978-1-7866-0804-8
ISBN: PB 978-1-7866-0805-5

Library of Congress Cataloging-in-Publication Data

Names: Culbertson, Carolyn, 1982- author.
Title: Words underway : continental philosophy of language / Carolyn Culbertson.
Description: London ; New York : Rowman & Littlefield International, 2019. | Includes bibliographi-
    cal references and index.
Identifiers: LCCN 2019003235 (print) | LCCN 2019018336 (ebook) | ISBN 9781786608062 (elec-
    tronic) | ISBN 9781786608048 (cloth : alk. paper) | ISBN 9781786608055 (pbk. : alk. paper)
Subjects: LCSH: Language and languages--Philosophy.
Classification: LCC P107 (ebook) | LCC P107 .C85 2019 (print) | DDC 401--dc23
LC record available at https://lccn.loc.gov/2019003235

Printed in the United States of America

Contents

Acknowledgments

This project is the culmination of several years of work spent developing and refining the arguments contained in this study. During this process, I have relied on different forms of support provided to me by many people. This book would not have been possible without their support, and any success that I enjoy from it is due to them.

First, I owe a significant debt to my teachers for both inspiring in me the love of wisdom that first turned me into a philosopher and instilling in me the patience and courage needed to follow the *logos*, wherever it may lead. Although several people over the years helped to foster this development, two deserve special mention by name. Jason Wirth first inspired me to study philosophy and first impressed upon me the critical-historical perspective that I needed to take myself seriously as a writer and a thinker. As a first-generation college student arriving in Atlanta, eager to broaden my intellectual horizons, I was fortunate indeed to have him as a mentor. The graduate faculty at the University of Oregon with whom I worked while a doctoral student not only helped deepen that critical-historical perspective, but also instilled in me a commitment to submit my philosophical work to rigorous self-assessment. I am particularly indebted to John Lysaker in this regard. As a seminar leader and my dissertation adviser, John helped tremendously in my development as a professional philosopher. He helped me to see that it is not enough for a philosophical argument to be radical; it should also be articulated clearly, so that others can follow along with the *logos* each step of the way and gauge the import of the argument for their lives. John also gave me the courage to believe that, if we can achieve clarity of this kind in our philosophical work, then we can move more freely around the discipline rather than alienating ourselves through hyper-specialization. John models this clarity and free mobility of thought in his seminars, in conversation, and in his writing, and I have benefited greatly from the model he provides.

Next, I am indebted to several colleagues who have directly or indirectly contributed to the formation of this book. I began having conversations about the project with members of the Heidegger Circle back in 2013 when I presented an early version of chapter 6 at the annual meeting that year in New Haven, Connecticut. Since then, several conversations within the Heidegger Circle, particularly with Emilia Angelova, Dan Dahlstrom, Bret Davis, Larry Hatab, Brendan Mahoney, and Karen Robertson, have helped shape different aspects of the project. Michael Naas also generously read and provided feedback on an early version of chapter 6. I thank Charles Bambach for inviting me to deliver a paper at the North Texas Heidegger Symposium in 2017 and giving me a chance to share a version of chapter 1 with this wonderful group. Conversations with Jennifer Gaffney and Ted George at that meeting were especially helpful for the development of the project. Finally, I am thankful to the North American Society for Philosophical Hermeneutics for supporting and encouraging my work since 2016 and for the opportunity to present a version of chapter 4 at the 2018 meeting in Naperville, Illinois. I thank David Ingram and Cynthia Nielsen in particular for their helpful feedback at that meeting. At times, I think I would have liked to complete this book more quickly, but when I consider how much it has been enriched by these conversations over the past five years—conversations with philosophers whose own work I admire—I am glad that I allowed the project to develop at the pace that it did.

Next, I want to acknowledge the tremendous support that I have received from the incredible community of colleagues and students I have at Florida Gulf Coast University. My understanding of Continental philosophy of language has benefited substantially from seminars on Butler, Gadamer, and feminist philosophy that I have offered at FGCU and from the students who worked diligently in these seminars with me. The precociousness and tireless work ethic of students like Elizabeth Portella and Rachel Cicoria pushed me to make the most out of these courses. My research assistant, Tirza Ben-Ezzer, was also a great help, and chapters 3 and 4 are particularly improved by conversations with her throughout the spring and summer of 2018. Dongjing Kang, my colleague in communication studies, has been a helpful interlocutor for me, and I have valued especially her insights as a reader of Gadamer. My colleagues in philosophy—Kevin Aho, Mohamad Al-Hakim, Landon Frim, Miles Hentrup, and Glenn Whitehouse—have been a constant source of support, encouragement, and inspiration. Their own projects as philosophers have challenged and inspired me, and collaborations with them over the years have helped to give shape to the philosophical perspective from which this book is written. I am profoundly thankful to have them all as colleagues. Beyond this, I want to give special acknowledgment to Kevin Aho for the helpful conversations about Heidegger over the years, and to Miles Hentrup for helping me think through the epistemological dimensions of this project and for the fastidious comments he provided on each chapter.

Finally, I have to thank a few people who have helped sustain me personally as I have labored through this project and who have cared for, and in many cases anticipated, my needs along the way. I doubt that I could have completed this book in a timely fashion without advice I received on the writing process from Hamad Al-Rayes. Beyond this, I have relied very much on the professional mentorship of Erin McCarthy, whose guidance on the writing process and on the personal dimensions of integrating feminism into the Continental and Comparative philosophical traditions impacted me at just the right time in my career. As is so often the case with professional achievements, the completion of this book would not have been possible without the support of my family. Their patience with my writing schedule and with the many other professional obligations that I juggle has lightened the burden of meeting these demands. I am thankful especially to my mother, not only for the loving patience she has shown as I have become busier and busier over the years, but for understanding and reaffirming for me why the work is worth it. Lastly, I owe a tremendous debt to Miles, who for the past twelve years has been my primary partner in philosophical dialogue and in almost every other aspect of my life. He has known just when to encourage my ideas and when to challenge them, when to motivate me in this project and when to help me step away from it, and I have benefited profoundly from his love and care.

A NOTE ABOUT THE TEXT

Three of the chapters in this book are modified versions of articles published elsewhere. I am grateful to the presses in each case for permission to reuse material for this project.

Chapter 1, "Walker Percy, Phenomenology, and the Mystery of Language," was originally published in *Walker Percy, Philosopher*, edited by Leslie Marsh (2018). It is reproduced with the permission of Palgrave Macmillan.

Chapter 5, "The Omnipotent Word of Medical Diagnosis and the Silence of Depression," was originally published in *IJFAB: International Journal of Feminist Approaches to Bioethics 9*, no. 1 (2016): 1–26. It is reproduced with the permission of University of Toronto Press.

Chapter 6, "Language as Habitat: Doing Justice to Experiences of Linguistic Alienation," was originally published as "My Language Which Is Not My Own: Heidegger and Derrida on the Ambiguity of Linguistic Life" in *Southwest Philosophy Review 32*, no. 2 (2016): 115–36.

Introduction

Language is a technological invention, an artificial product that humans first started to develop many thousands of years ago and have been gradually transforming ever since. Spoken language is thought to have first evolved around 100,000 years ago, although the date is very difficult to determine. Written language first emerged in ancient Sumer about 5,000 years ago. The invention of the printing press came about in Europe in the fifteenth century and in China 600 years earlier. Meanwhile, new communication technologies continue to emerge and impact the evolution of this human invention. Indeed, while in our everyday lives we tend not to bring to mind its artificial character, there is arguably no more significant invention in human history than the invention of language.

To emphasize the artificiality of language by pointing to its history, however, should not keep us from recognizing how integral language has become to the human mode of being. The acquisition of language fundamentally changes the way that we experience and understand the world—a change that, while unobservable as an event in the evolution of the human species, is readily observable during early childhood. Language acquisition provides children with a wealth of concepts that add depth and richness to the landscape of their thoughts. Language allows them to reference objects that are not immediately present. It also allows for a number of second-order operations, including reflection on, description of, and analysis of those objects. Moreover, in acquiring language, children develop the capacity for constructing narratives, something that will prove important as they work throughout their lives to develop and refine their understanding of the world and of themselves. The narratives and the concepts that they develop, moreover, will transform and deepen the bonds they have with others, as they will learn the stories and the ideas that matter most in their discourse communities. Finally, children learn an array of performative speech acts—how to say "no," to apologize, to promise—that very soon become pivotal to their social interactions. Over time, they no longer relate to language as some external artifice. Language becomes something much more intimate. The child becomes *a linguistic being*.

We can better understand this point if we compare this process and its result to the learning of a musical instrument, say, a piano. The piano is an artificial object, a fact that is undeniable to the person just learning to play, to whom its technique is not yet intuitive. For the novice, nothing about the technique feels natural or spontaneous. Yet over time this changes. After years of practice, the technique comes much more naturally. The same thing applies to learning language. Just like the piano that finally feels comfortable with time, words eventually feel to us like the natural expression of our feelings, thoughts, and perceptions.

Moreover, for the linguistic being, the words of others start to carry great strength as well. Listening to or reading another's words, we may find ourselves struck by how perfectly these capture something we had only imperfectly apprehended before. Such moments are among the most precious. The nineteenth-century American philosopher Ralph Waldo Emerson, makes this point in "The American Scholar" when he describes how an audience takes pleasure in listening to a speech that seems to "fulfill for them their own nature." "The people delight in it," Emerson writes, "the better part of every man feels, This is my music; this is myself."[1] The capacity for such delight in another's words reveals what an intimate part of our lives this invention has become.

This is, however, only half of the story, for while language can and often does appear to people this way—fulfilling for us our own nature— it can also be a source of alienation. In trying to give expression to some experience, we sometimes find words skewed, inadequate, or inexplicably difficult to interpret. At other times, we might feel shame or embarrassment at words we have spoken, confronted by unintended meanings that persist beyond our control. There are times when, despite a sincere attempt to communicate, we feel we have not been fully understood and other times when, despite a sincere effort to listen, we feel we are not able to fully understand. For instance, in Plato's *Meno*, the title character breaks down in frustration at one point after Socrates brings to light problems with the understanding of virtue that he has presented. Likening Socrates to a torpedo fish that numbs whomever it comes into contact with, Meno laments the way in which he suddenly feels perplexed by the dialogue with Socrates: "Yet I have made many speeches about virtue before large audiences on a thousand occasions, very good speeches I thought, but now I cannot even say what it is."[2] Here Meno, who is used to being able to speak and dialogue with others about the topic of virtue very comfortably, suddenly feels like a stranger to himself.

Such alienation can be momentary—marked by acute frustration or embarrassment—but it can also be more chronic. "Words, words, words," Hamlet famously bemoans to Polonius, despairing in his melancholic state over how words can cover the truth and even conspire with political deception. Even those who do not see themselves as sharing Hamlet's gloomy disposition may feel something similar in other situations. For instance, some might regard an entire conversation that would otherwise make a claim on them to be fundamentally worthless because of some ideological baggage or blind spot they believe to be shared by those involved in the deliberation. They give up on dialoguing with others. For them, the terms of the deliberation have been stacked against any genuine disclosure. Alternatively, others might come to feel chronic alienation from language if their attempts to communicate routinely fail, as can happen in cases of trauma or simply when nobody really listens to them. In these situations, language no longer operates like the piano we have learned to play with naturalness and spontaneity. It becomes a source of frustration.

That experiences like these can be so frustrating bespeaks the importance of language for our existence. It is the distinctive mode of human existence as linguistic being that makes experiences like these not only frustrating but *alienating* for us—alienating because they unsettle our very mode of existence. As linguistic beings, language is our natural habitat. It is our primary way of making sense of the world, including ourselves. Because of this, we struggle mightily—even existentially— when our habitual way of dwelling in language is upset.

WHY CONTINENTAL PHILOSOPHY OF LANGUAGE?

Despite the deep impact that such experiences can have on our lives, scholars of the philosophy of language have paid little attention to them. There seem to be at least two reasons for this. First, such considerations fall outside of the traditional scope of their investigation. Linguists and philosophers of language alike have traditionally taken the object of their investigations to be the secure possession of a collective group of speakers, a system whereby meanings or (in speech-act theory) social functions are made immediately available to all members of that group. Benjamin Lee Whorf, for example, famously argued that "we cut nature up, organize it into concepts, and ascribe significances as we do, largely because we are parties to an agreement to organize it in this way—an agreement that holds throughout our speech community and is codified in the patterns of our language."[3] Implicit in the very model of language that such theorists are working with, then, is the assumption that speakers of a language maintain a consistent, unchanging relationship to that language, and that this relationship is identical for all speakers of that language. Within the parameters of this model, then, little attention is paid to the potential for members of that collective group to feel alienated from language and to the existential struggle that can unfold as they work through that alienation.

Second, over the past century, many philosophers have developed an epistemological commitment to resolving philosophical questions by turning to language as it is understood on the model just described. This development is often referred to as the "linguistic turn" in philosophy.[4] For linguistic turn philosophers, the system of language becomes the means by which philosophical questions must be resolved. As such, the model of language as a collectively possessed system of meaning is reinforced not only as a description of ordinary language use, but as a paradigm for what is intelligible. As a result, the commitment to this model strengthens and becomes more intentional. Whereas Whorf claimed only that people have a tendency to understand the universe through a shared system of meaning but allowed for the possibility that we might "frame a new language by which to adjust itself to a wider universe,"[5] Richard Rorty argues that no such deviation from the system is possible. Philosophy, he argues, must renounce the metaphysical ambitions that have characterized the tradition up to this point and to concentrate its efforts, if it intends to go on at all as a science, solely on developing understanding within the confines of a particular idiom.[6] In this context, any exploration of the human ability to become alienated from language would become immediately suspect on epistemological grounds. A speaker of a language could not actually relate to the world as an epistemological subject except by means of that system of meaning held in common with fellow speakers of that language.[7]

For these reasons, little attention has been given to the phenomenon of linguistic alienation in the literature that typically comprises what we call "philosophy of language." By contrast, the theme of linguistic alienation and, more generally, the vicissitudes of the linguistic being's relationship to language, has been central to conversations about language in the Continental tradition. In their writings on language, Continental philosophers like Jacques Derrida, Hans-Georg Gadamer, and Julia Kristeva pay special attention to cases of language in which some form of alienation is at work, for example, when we are confronted with a text that seems to resist our codified patterns of interpretation, or when we have a persistent sense that the sadness we feel is beyond words. Moreover, rather than focusing just on language as a self-enclosed, continuous, unchanging system that codifies a certain way of understanding the world, Continental philosophers examine language as it arises in the task of human existence and as a means by which we are constantly revising *what* we understand and *how* we understand.

It is not surprising, then, that the work of Continental philosophers has rarely been considered part of the philosophy of language as a discipline. Inevitably, readings by Russell, Frege, and Quine are found in the anthologies assigned in philosophy of language classes. One does *not* find readings by Heidegger, Gadamer, or Derrida, although each understood the theme of language to be central to their philosophical work. Important contributions on the theme of language made by feminist or postcolonial philosophers, perspectives that are now regularly in conversation with phenomenology and hermeneutics, will not be found in these books either.

These omissions are notable and not just because contributions on the topic from some of the most influential philosophers of the past century are left out. More importantly, by omitting Continental authors from the conversation, we are excluding those accounts that deal most extensively with linguistic alienation and other intricacies of the human relationship to language. The phenomenon of linguistic alienation becomes largely invisible. Yet, people can and often do feel alienated from language, as, for example, Denise Riley does when she reports: "When I write *I* and follow up the pronoun with a self-description, feelings of fraud grip me."[8] Such an experience cannot be accounted for by those who view language as a finite set of concepts that exhaustively determines and coordinates the way a group of people understands the world, just as it cannot account for the much more felicitous experience of discovering words (our own or another's) that suddenly speak to us, making things clear. Yet such experiences, be they uplifting or deflating, tend to impact our lives profoundly.

This leads me to the second reason why the omission of Continental philosophy from the conversation is of concern and why its inclusion is important. When one thinks about language as a static system of meaning that one necessarily has in place by virtue of membership in a particular speech community, it becomes impossible to see how the understanding of a linguistic being is always evolving. Instead, one takes how and what the speaking subject understands to be as fixed as the system of language itself. By contrast, if one takes seriously the vicissitudes of linguistic life described above as cognitively significant moments, then it becomes clear that understanding is not reducible to a static set of concepts, but is a process always underway.

The tendency to exclude the topic of alienation from the philosophy of language based on the epistemological concern mentioned above, then, is unwarranted. It is not the case that a person relates to the world as an epistemological subject only when employing a static system of meaning codified in the patterns of language agreed upon by that person's speech community. Philosophical investigations that explore the vicissitudes of linguistic life, then, should not be excluded from the field of the philosophy of language on epistemological grounds, but rather should be taken to shed new light on basic epistemological questions.

CULTIVATING THE TRADITION

In light of these concerns, *Words Underway* aims to do three things: to provide a narrative that helps readers see how Continental philosophy of language developed over the past century and why it developed in this way; to examine the role of linguistic alienation in this development; and, finally, to clarify the conception of understanding that develops in the tradition, in part, as a response to the phenomenon of linguistic alienation. Let me elaborate on each of these objectives.

First, then, the book aims to give an account of some of the significant contributions that Continental philosophers have made to the philosophy of language. Rather than examining how Continental philosophers have answered the questions posed by Anglo-American philosophers of language, though, and thus working within the terrain that they have mapped, the book aspires to show how Continental philosophers of language have mapped out the terrain themselves. I begin by examining the approach to language taken by early-twentieth century phenomenologist Martin Heidegger, a seminal figure for the Continental tradition. In chapter 1, I explain how Heidegger's non-dualistic analysis of being-in-the-world and the concomitant structure of worldhood brings to light the centrality of language for the human mode of existence, that is, for both our way of being-in-the-world and for worldhood itself. This analysis, I explain, was groundbreaking not only for later Continental thinkers like Hans-Georg Gadamer, but also for literary writers like Walker Percy, who drew from Heidegger in his own essays on language. In chapter 2, I consider the development that takes place in Heidegger's own thought, where in his later work he begins to focus on encounters with what I call non-immediate language, that is, speech that isn't ready-to-hand but pulls us up short in some way, perhaps even alienating us from the everyday mode of our linguistic being. This can happen, for example, with a dialogue that requires careful listening or with a text that demands close reading. I explore how this late focus for Heidegger becomes the central focus for Gadamer's hermeneutic philosophy of language, which examines the nature of the understanding that can result from such encounters, that is, that can unfold when we encounter words underway. Chapter 3, then, takes up how this interest in linguistic alienation and non-immediate language develops more concretely in the context of Continental philosophy's engagement with post-Holocaust literature. I argue that this literature appears to Derrida as precisely that non-immediate language that requires careful listening and reflection. I mark this as a significant point in the development of Continental philosophy of language, where the tradition begins to recognize the normative significance of understanding the speech of the other, particularly when, as in the case of trauma survivors, their language retreats into non-immediacy; and where the tradition begins to see clearly the ethical stakes of knowing how to approach the task of understanding in such cases. In chapters 4 and 5, I explore how both points later become significant topics of investigation within Continental feminist philosophy. Here I look at discussions within Continental feminism about the origins of, the significance of, and the proper response to women's silence. In chapter 4, I consider some of the important parallels between the hermeneutic account of language discussed in chapter 2 and the work of Judith Butler and Sandra Bartky on linguistic being and linguistic alienation. Here again I mark a moment where the conversation within the Continental tradition develops, explaining how Continental feminism pushes the broader tradition to say more about the social conditions that enable us to, or prevent us from, flourishing as linguistic beings. In chapter 5, I elaborate on this last point by examining Julia Kristeva's work on the origins of silence in cases of female depression and on the kind of therapeutic approach necessary to heal the linguistic subject in this case—an approach that, once again, has important parallels with the hermeneutic conception of understanding outlined earlier. Finally, in the last chapter of the book, I consider how Continental philosophers have dealt with the metahistorical question of whether philosophy, or thought, remains bound to the historical discourses that we inherit. With this question I return first, to Heidegger's work to examine the relationship between the historical and linguistic aspects of our being, and second, to Derrida's reflections on the colonial history of the French language in order to highlight the normative significance of Heidegger's analysis.

In mapping out this terrain, my hope, then, is to help bring more awareness to the existence of a distinctive tradition of philosophical inquiry into language and to the important questions, arguments, and problematics that have been developed within this tradition over the past century. That said, my project in this book is not to undertake a comprehensive survey of every text and argument considered at some point significant by Continental thinkers. As will become clear in my final chapter, I find such an approach to history suspicious. I do not approach the tradition of Continental philosophy as something to be understood by simply deciphering the past independently from any reflection on the present. Instead, I take "tradition" here in Gadamer's sense of the word— as something never simply in the past, but also always in progress. As Gadamer puts it, tradition "does not persist because of the inertia of what once existed" but "needs to be affirmed, embraced, cultivated" in the present.[9] This is, then, the secondary meaning of the title of this book. *Words Underway* refers not only to the ongoing task of understanding that we are always engaged in as linguistic beings. It also serves to remind readers that what is referenced in the subtitle, Continental philosophy of language, is itself a tradition still underway.

My second aim in this book is to bring attention to and shed light on the phenomenon of linguistic alienation and its significance for understanding our mode of being. Because we do not tend to recognize the ontological significance of language, we do not tend to recognize the kind of suffering that occurs when language ceases to function normally for a person. As I argue in chapter 3, though, the suffering experienced by survivors of trauma is often compounded by the collapse of their normal relationship to language. As Elaine Scarry argues, this is what many survivors of torture struggle with, survivors who have undergone the trauma of having their voices instrumentalized against them or otherwise broken down. Scarry describes how torture often operates by "breaking off the voice, making it their own, making it speak their words, making it cry when they want it to cry, be silent when they want its silence."[10] Linguistic alienation can be used intentionally as a means of manipulation in this way. It can also, however, emerge gradually and in a different form through the roles one learns to play in the communicative exchanges that occur in normalized social relations. In chapter 5, I argue that it is the gradual adoption of such a role that leads so many women into a state of depression where they become detached from language, where their speech becomes to them, as Kristeva says, "like an alien skin."[11] Such examples help us to see how profoundly unsettling linguistic alienation can be and, hence, how important it is to think through the relationship to language that is compromised in such situations.

Yet I will insist that, in another sense, alienation is intrinsic to our relationship to language and comprises part of what makes linguistic activity so important to human fulfillment. When we encounter language that pulls us up short, we are compelled to be more attentive to what we are trying to understand and, in turn, more reflective on and potentially critical of our habitual ways of recognizing and interpreting what we encounter. Such experiences make us question precisely those habits that Whorf describes as agreed-upon patterns of conceptualization encoded in our system of language. Undoubtedly, such experiences alienate us temporarily from our linguistic milieu, but alienation in this sense, as Gadamer reminds us, is a normal part of the process of reading a text and engaging in genuine conversation with another.[12] Participating in a conversation, after all, requires that we continually adjust the meaning inevitably projected on the basis of our own linguistic habits in an attempt to understand what is being said. Likewise, readers of a text must be willing to suspend some of their normal habits of interpretation that they inevitably bring with them as readers in order to follow along with what is actually being said in a text. In these cases, becoming alienated from the language as a ready-to-hand source of meaning is not a source of suffering. On the contrary, as Derrida makes clear in his commentary on Paul Celan, such an experience can, in fact, strengthen the claim that a text makes on its readers.[13] Moreover, insofar as it enables us to be fascinated and moved by something that we hear or that we read, it is part of what gives us joy as linguistic beings.

Alienation in this sense ought to be distinguished from the first form of alienation described. The first form occurs when one's linguistic being is jeopardized, and in a way that causes extreme suffering. Within the Continental tradition, it is this form of linguistic alienation that is often and rightfully the object of normative critique. The second type of alienation, by contrast, is regularly valued by Continental philosophers. Although emphasizing the importance of both can create confusion at times, both forms of alienation are important to consider and, indeed, I argue, must even be considered in relation to one another. It is important, after all, to resist oppressive forms of social organization that leave people alienated from language (their voices, for example, silenced or instrumentalized against them), but we run into trouble if we think that the ultimate goal of such resistance should be to restore for people a relationship to language that is fully immediate, without the possibility of ever having their linguistically embedded habits of thinking challenged in dialogue with another. This sort of goal, after all, would be ethically and politically problematic in that it would mean shutting people off from other voices that have yet to speak and be understood, that await participation in the living system of language. More primordially, it would be problematic in that our openness to dialogue with the other and the critical self-relation that such openness entails are intrinsic parts of our linguistic being. Without this openness, we become creatures of a different kind.

This leads me to the third and final aim of this book, which is epistemological in character. I want to give an account of the concept of understanding that develops in Continental philosophy as it grapples with the topic of language and, in particular, with linguistic alienation. Moreover, I want to demonstrate why theorizing from the standpoint of linguistic alienation in either sense described above needn't mean undermining our basis for knowledge. I will argue that experiences of being pulled up short by language play a positive role in the development of understanding, conceived of as an ongoing historical process continually responsive to the particularities of the situations in which it operates. There are times, after all, when my ability to understand depends on my ability to put these rules at risk, to suspend them as needed—to listen, in other words, in a different way. This is the kind of understanding that Continental philosophers like Derrida learned to cultivate in reading poetry written by survivors of the trauma of the Holocaust. It is also the kind of understanding that Kristeva practices in her work as a clinical therapist, even when her patient seems to have withdrawn completely from his or her linguistic being. In such cases, if I want to understand what is being said, I must not assume that I immediately know the point my interlocutor is making as soon as the first sentence is uttered. I need to keep my interpretation in suspense until the right time, lest impatience prevents me from really listening.

No mastery of language can fill in gaps like these. They are integral, for one thing, to the system of human communication. As Kristeva writes, "Our gift of speech, of situating ourselves in time for an other, could exist nowhere except beyond an abyss. Speaking beings, from their ability to endure in time up to their enthusiastic, learned, or simply amusing constructions, demand a break, a renunciation, an unease at their foundations."[14] Kristeva's point here contests a dominant conception of language today. We often assume that human languages work in the same way that computer programming languages do, as though knowing how to communicate entails nothing more than possessing technical knowledge of fixed linguistic rules. What we mean by a "language" in speaking about such artificial languages, though, is a technical means of communicating orders to a recipient. Understanding, in this context, means simply performing the action intended by the speaker—for instance, when a computer performs the action intended by the programmer—preferably without any of the long pauses (pauses for listening, for self-examination, etc.) that tend to punctuate all points in the process of human communication. The comparison may hold when viewed at the level of certain individual speech acts like "please come here" or "I am ready to go." Indeed, such statements are the first ones that new speakers of a language are able to master with the rudimentary skills that they have. But when we step back and consider the larger picture of human communication, we find that the comparison is limited.

It is not only that such a model is inadequate for understanding language and communication. It is also inadequate for understanding the nature of understanding. This is because, for one, it discourages us from seeing how understanding develops over time and, in part, through experiences of having one's linguistically embedded habits of thought challenged. This has led Continental philosophers like Butler to insist on the cognitive import of precisely those moments where it would seem that language fails us. For Butler, this is the cognitive import of critique. As Butler puts it:

> One asks about the limits of ways of knowing because one has already run up against a crisis within the epistemological field in which one lives. The categories by which social life is ordered produce a certain incoherence or entire realms of unspeakability. And it is from this condition, the tear in the fabric of our epistemological web, that the practice of critique emerges.[15]

If Butler is right to identify such an experience as the impetus for the epistemological operation of critique, and thus as a positive moment in the development of understanding, then we can easily see why the computer model of human understanding fails. Computers aren't pulled up short. They can experience neither the "crisis within the epistemological field in which one lives" nor the satisfaction of regaining a coherent understanding of what had become incoherent. Yet such vicissitudes are a constant feature of our existence as human beings, and they are what we must inevitably bear as we seek to refine our understanding of the world.

There are several important reasons, then, for taking more seriously the contributions that the Continental tradition has made to the philosophy of language, as I hope the investigation that follows makes clear. That said, readers of this book needn't approach it with any interest in the Continental tradition per se, for the problematics explored in the book are of widespread and, I think, clear importance for all of us today. As a whole, we think too little today about the importance of language in human life. We put little stock in the kind of understanding that develops through dialogue with our contemporaries and even less in the kind that develops, through reading and writing, in dialogue with the past. We denigrate such processes as irrational, because they emerge in response to ideas already underway rather than presuming to investigate from scratch, without presupposition. This has troubling implications for our attitudes toward public discourse and, of course, for the fate of the humanities, in which the art of such understanding has traditionally been fostered.

In general, we give little thought to the social conditions that foster our flourishing as linguistic beings or even that provide us with a sense that we have a "voice" in our communities. Yet the legitimacy of many social arrangements, including modern liberal democracies, depends on participants having a voice in that society's deliberative process—something that requires a sense of political efficacy and a sense that their voice matters to the formation of their culture. We need to think more seriously, then, about what enables people to regard themselves as meaningful participants in the discourses that play a constitutive role in their worlds, and about the suffering that can occur when they are unable to regard themselves as such.

These are widespread and pressing concerns that have come increasingly to light for me in reading Continental philosophy over the past decade and a half. It is in view of such concerns as well, then, that I invite readers to explore the terrain mapped out by Continental philosophers of language and to see for themselves what light it can shed on these problems today.

NOTES

1. Ralph Waldo Emerson, "The American Scholar," in *Emerson: Essays and Poems* (New York: Library of America, 1996), 97.

2. Plato, "Meno," in *Plato: Complete Works*, ed. John M. Cooper (Indianapolis, IN: Hackett, 1997), 879 (80a).

3. Benjamin Lee Whorf, "Science and Linguistics," in *Language, Thought, and Reality: Selected Writings of Benjamin Lee Whorf* (Cambridge, MA: MIT Press, 1956), 213.

4. Richard Rorty, "Introduction," in *The Linguistic Turn: Essays in Philosophical Method* (Chicago: University of Chicago Press, 1967), 1–40.

5. Benjamin Lee Whorf, "The Relation of Habitual Thought and Behavior to Language," in *Language, Thought, and Reality: Selected Writings of Benjamin Lee Whorf* (Cambridge, MA: MIT Press, 1956), 154.

6. Rorty, "Introduction," *The Linguistic Turn*.

7. For an earlier version of this argument, see G. E. Moore's "A Defence of Common Sense," in *Contemporary British Philosophy*, ed. J. H. Muirhead (London: George Allen and Unwin, 1925), 192–233.

8. Denise Riley, "Linguistic Unease," in *The Words of Selves: Identification, Solidarity, Irony* (Palo Alto, CA: Stanford University Press, 2000), 59.

9. Hans-Georg Gadamer, *Truth and Method*, trans. Joel Weinsheimer and Donald G. Marshall (London: Bloomsbury, 2004), 293.

10. Elaine Scarry, *The Body in Pain: The Making and Unmaking of the World* (Oxford: Oxford University Press, 1985), 54.

11. Julia Kristeva, *Black Sun: Depression and Melancholia*, trans. Leon S. Roudiez (New York: Columbia University Press, 1989), 53.

12. Whorf, "The Relation of Habitual Thought and Behavior to Language"; Gadamer, *Truth and Method*, 407.

13. Jacques Derrida, "Shibboleth," in *Sovereignties in Question: The Poetics of Paul Celan*, ed. Thomas Dutoit and Outi Pasanen (New York: Fordham University Press, 2005), 1–64.

14. Kristeva, *Black Sun*, 42.

15. Judith Butler, "What Is Critique?: An Essay on Foucault's Virtue," in *The Political: Readings in Continental Philosophy*, ed. David Ingram (London: Blackwell, 2002), 215.

ONE

Walker Percy, Phenomenology, and the Mystery of Language

The idea that language is what most distinguishes the human being as a species has been around for a very long time. In his *Nicomachean Ethics*, the ancient Greek philosopher, Aristotle, describes the human being as *zōon logon echon*, the animal that has language (*logos*).[1] Aristotle thought the capacity for language so important to human life that no person could truly flourish in his being without actively putting it to work through reasoning and deliberation. Indeed, despite the well-known antagonism between philosophers and rhetoricians of ancient Greece, it is worth remembering what the two sides had in common: philosophers and rhetoricians alike believed strongly in the power of speech to rightly guide both individual and city.

This way of understanding the human being seems to have been about as intuitively right for the philosophers of ancient Greece as it is today intuitively wrong for us moderns. Whenever I have introduced this idea to students in philosophy classes, I have unfailingly heard the same objections. Students inevitably will have heard of scientific studies about how animals communicate with one another, so they conclude that an old thinker like Aristotle must have come to a faulty conclusion based on the fact that he did not have access to these scientific studies. Birds clearly send songs to one another; other birds understand and respond to those songs. Humans have even trained some animals to communicate with them. Chimpanzees use hand signals. Even pet dogs are often trained by their human companions to understand a range of different words. The idea, then, that language is the most distinctively human trait seems thoroughly unconvincing.

From this perspective, the very idea of *philosophy of language* makes little sense. After all, if one wants to understand how language works, then it seems that one ought to just observe what happens—mentally or behaviorally—when a person learns a word, hears and understands a sentence, successfully makes a request of another, and so forth. With this model, the measure of successful communication in each case would be an observable effect independent of the linguistic world: Did the dog go fetch when it heard the human's command? Did the request for salt successfully yield the salt? In other words, it seems that we can understand how language works just fine by approaching it as a process that can be broken up into a series of observable events—some that we observe within the subject, others that we observe in the world outside of the subject. Understood along these lines, it seems like the tools of science are perfectly adequate for the task, while philosophy is unnecessary for it.

But is this model appropriate for thinking about everything that human beings do with language? As I write these words, for example, I know that there will be no readily observable effects, no appearance of products to serve as a clear measure for gauging the success of what I am writing. Hannah Arendt was right on this point: the activity of human speech in this sense is not about the fabrication of products at all.[2] What fuels a writer is something else. A writer would like to say something that has not been said—to prompt the reader to think about things in a new way. Writers would like to contribute to the development of new understanding. As you read this paragraph, for example, what I hope is happening is not just what transpires when a dog goes to fetch upon hearing a human's command. No, the task of understanding for the reader is clearly different. So is the task of listening to another in conversation. We humans delight in those conversations that take us to unexpected places, just as we delight in the book that says something different each time we read it. It would seem that this sort of activity that we participate in as linguistic beings requires a *philosophical* examination, since the theoretical model sketched above is not capable of accounting for it.

Yet it should not be surprising that it was perhaps a writer, not a specialist in the discipline of philosophy, who expressed the need for a philosophical examination of language most powerfully. In addition to his novels, over the course of his lifetime the Louisiana writer Walker Percy wrote dozens of theoretical essays examining the subject of language. He studied major developments in linguistics and the philosophy of language taking place in the twentieth century, an undertaking that, by his own account, became a "mild obsession" of his during the 1960s and 1970s. But it was Percy's craft as a writer that especially motivated his interest in the topic. As a writer, Percy experienced a persistent sense of wonder about something that we usually take for granted. This is simply, as he puts it, "what happens when people talk, when one person names something or says a sentence about something and another person understands him."[3] As a novelist, of course, Percy very well might have refrained from such investigations—submitting to the muse of writing without questioning the grounds and the ends of his own craft. Or, he could have limited his readings to the field of literary theory, focusing on language only in its literary mode. Instead, for decades he diligently examined many of the most important contributions to linguistics and the philosophy of language during his lifetime.

As many commentators have pointed out, Percy found the writings of Charles Sanders Peirce particularly illuminating and drew a good deal from Peirce's semiotic theory in his own writing.[4] But Percy was also one of the first major intellectual figures in the United States to recognize the importance of insights from Continental philosophers exploring the nature of language. Percy's essays on language reference not only figures like Rudolf Carnap, Noam Chomsky, and Alfred Tarski, but also Ludwig Binswanger, Martin Buber, Martin Heidegger, Søren Kierkegaard, Gabriel Marcel, Jean-Paul Sartre, and George Steiner. This was not typical for the time. Much like today, philosophy of language during the 1960s and 1970s was associated almost exclusively with Anglo-American philosophy. In this context, Percy's engagement with the Continental tradition is notable. Moreover, Percy's essays on language manage to capture some of Continental philosophy's most important insights into what is distinctive about human linguistic activity, what is essential about the role of language for our existence, and what it is that keeps us from recognizing these things today. In this chapter, then, I would like to introduce these three key insights by way of Percy's writing and the early phenomenology of Martin Heidegger, which influenced Percy.

THE PECULIAR LIFE OF THE LINGUISTIC BEING

That language plays an essential role in our existence should be obvious. We are constantly engaging with language in some way or another. We do this not only when speaking, listening, writing, or reading, but even in the silence of our thoughts, when we are in dialogue with ourselves. Moreover, most of our social interactions are mediated by language in some way—be it in formal ways as in written laws and verbal contracts or in informal ways as in the customary verbal exchanges that we engage in every day with friends, family members, coworkers, neighbors, and so on. Yet, as Percy explains, this situation does not make it easier for us to understand the integral role of language in our lives. "The difficulty," he writes, "is that it *is* under our noses; it is too close and too familiar. Language, symbolization, is the stuff of which our knowledge and awareness of the world are made, the medium through which we see the world. Trying to see it is like trying to see the mirror by which we see everything else."[5] Percy devises several schemes for this purpose. In his essay, "The Delta Factor," for example, he invites us to view human behavior through the eyes of a Martian who has come to earth to study human beings. The first thing that would stand out to the visitor about our behavior, Percy explains, is how constantly we humans are involved with linguistic activity in some way.

> Imagine the Martian's astonishment after landing when he observes that earthlings talk all the time or otherwise traffic in symbols: gossip, tell jokes, argue, make reports, deliver lectures, listen to lectures, take notes, write books, read books, paint pictures, look at pictures, stage plays, attend plays, tell stories, listen to stories, cover blackboards with math symbols—and even at night dream dreams that are a very tissue of symbols.[6]

Now, Percy's description of human behavior makes two things clear. First, the description is clearly meant to show how frequently all of us are engaged in linguistic activity of some kind. We are engaged not only when we are producing statements as physical utterances, but also when we are absorbed in a book, when we are dreaming, when we are engaged in abstract symbolization, and so on. In each case we are interpreting, using, and in some cases helping to formulate signs with shared meanings. Indeed, one is even "speaking" in this sense when one chooses to keep silent, say, as an expression of defiance or frustration. The sheer amount of time that we spend engaged in such activity already suggests that language plays a distinctive role in our lives, and this is something—as Percy points out—even a Martian could understand very plainly about human behavior from observation alone. What may be harder to notice, though, is that we are actually engaged in linguistic activity toward a variety of ends. We "traffic in symbols" in order to deepen our understanding, to articulate formal truths, for amusement, for humor, for artistic expression, for the sake of dialogue with others, and so on. This is one way in which our relationship to language is distinct—one way that the human can be said to be *zōon logon echon*, the linguistic being, and not just a creature for whom language serves some single, limited purpose.

Indeed, many of these ends to which we put language in fact depend on language, and would not exist without it. Take the activity of scientific inquiry. When we think of scientific inquiry, we are likely to focus on the interaction between a researcher and objects of research, say, in the natural world. We tend to see language as epiphenomenal in this context—something needed to coordinate among researchers and to communicate results, but not constitutive for the inquiry in any way. However, as Helen Longino has argued, the objects, models, and concepts with which science deals are inevitably social; they emerge from social discourse.[7] Moreover, as Charles P. Bigger explains, "The truth conditions for the human sciences lie within those conditions of language, essentially spiritual, which constitute knower and known, self and other, man and world. This is the great theme of the *logos* itself."[8] Scientific pursuits only take place, then, in a world where there is language. Likewise, there could be no pursuit of formal validity without a formal language like mathematics or logic with which to construct proofs. Similarly, there would be no artistic expression or humorous performances without a range of symbols—that is, signs with socially shared meanings—from which to draw. All of these pursuits draw from the social activity of language and would be incomprehensible without it. In light of this, we can see that language is not just a tool that can help us accomplish a number of ends; it is also, importantly, a source of ends itself.

This is why, for Percy, it is important to consider what a transformative event language acquisition is. The tendency, of course, is to think about what happens in this process as the gradual acquisition of a set of tools, and to imagine that the person learning a language is motivated to acquire these tools because they are instrumental to their existing goals. Certainly this is the most popular way of describing the rationale of language acquisition to adult language learners. For example, a common rationale given for teaching college-level reading and writing is that it provides a set of skills that are beneficial for communicating in the job place, in public discourse, in our interpersonal relationships, and so on. The message to students, then, is that working on college-level reading and writing is valuable only as a means—a means to perform more effectively in these spheres of action. A similar message is often given to students about the value of learning a foreign language. If language is itself a source of ends, though, these arguments leave out something important. They fail to do justice to the transformative and creative effect of reading and writing.

This transformative effect is even clearer when we consider what happens when a child starts to acquire language. No doubt part of what the child does in this process mirrors what the dog does when it learns words like "sit" and "heel." They learn to respond to certain verbal cues, and in the case of children, to give verbal cues that will typically produce one kind of response. Such learning is assisted by mirror neurons that are present in human and nonhuman animals alike.[9] The acquisition of language in this sense is important to the integration of the child into a community. In this way, it is instrumental for the child's survival. But the child is also undergoing something even more profound: entering into a veritable *world* of language. What does this mean? To talk about the development of language as the entrance into a new world in this sense means that, with this development, there is a fundamental transformation not only in how we think about the world, but even more fundamentally, in what appears to us and how it appears. Language's function becomes ontological rather than instrumental. Arendt likens this transformation to a "second birth."[10] Echoing this sentiment, Percy writes, "Once man has crossed the threshold of language and the use of other symbols, he literally lives in a new and different world."[11]

This development has no parallel in the nonhuman animal world. It distinguishes the human being from other animals, and makes it so that many of the concepts and models we use to understand the lives of other creatures fall short in explaining the human mode of being. As Percy explains:

> It, this strange new creature, not only has an environment, as do all creatures. It has a *world*. Its world is the totality of that which is named. This is different from its environment. An environment has gaps. There are no gaps in a world. Nectar is part of the environment of a bee. Cabbages and kings and Buicks are not. There are no gaps in the world of this new creature, because the gaps are called that, *gaps*, or *the unknown*, or out there, or *don't know*.[12]

It is this, then—the emergence of a linguistic world—that is distinctively human. When one has a linguistic world, one pushes for everything to have a place and meaning in language. In children, this is manifest as the desire to know the name for all things. In adults, it is the desire to expand one's understanding of this world through language—through the conversations one has, the books one reads, the jokes one hears, the letters one writes, and so on. The one who "has language" [*logon echon*] in this sense—the linguistic being—has it in a qualitatively different way than does a trained chimpanzee or, to be sure, a programmed computer.

This distinction is lost on us today, for the most part. Because of a tendency to equate reality strictly with that which the empirical sciences can explain, contemporary thinking rarely recognizes the linguistic world of the human being or its ontological function. If language is recognized, it is only the objective works produced through linguistic activity—bridges built, homework assignments submitted, medical discoveries made, computer programs designed. What goes unnoticed and unanalyzed, by contrast, is the linguistic world that leads us to these products, without which none of these things would matter or even exist. A study, for example, on the correlation between meditative practice and certain brain wave readings only matters given a number of discourses already in circulation, for example, about the problems of stress and the importance of self-care.

Again, it is easy to overlook how fundamental discourse is in our lives; as Percy explains, it is the medium through which our understanding is constantly taking place. To bring this medium into focus, it is helpful to think about how a person's life changes with the acquisition of language. A special case in point is the account that the famous writer, Helen Keller, gives of her experience learning how to speak as a young child who, due to illness, lost both her vision and her hearing in her second year of life. Percy is particularly fascinated with Keller's account of her experience, and at times attributes some of his most important insights into the question of language to Keller's story. What fascinates

Percy is, of course, the nature of the famous breakthrough Keller experienced as an eight-year-old child—a development that fundamentally changed the form of her existence and the role of language in it. Percy points out that, prior to this event, Keller had already possessed the ability to communicate basic messages with others. She could signal for a piece of cake when she wanted a piece of cake. She could use a set of symbols as tools to accomplish certain ends. It was not until that fateful day in 1887, however, that Keller developed a relationship to language that would eventually allow her to read, to lecture, to have conversations, and eventually to become an eloquent, sophisticated, and prodigious writer and activist—engaging with the important moral and political questions of the day. According to Keller's own account, the decisive moment occurred during a routine teaching procedure. Anne Sullivan and Keller were outside, and Sullivan, Keller's teacher, ran the young girl's hand under a stream of water from a spout, spelling the word "water" into her other hand. Keller recalls a "misty consciousness" coming upon her, revealing to her "the mystery of language." "I left the house eager to learn. Everything had a name, and each name gave birth to a new thought. As we returned to the house every object which I touched seemed to quiver with new life. That was because I saw everything with the strange, new sight that had come to me." [13]

For Percy, we can learn about what is distinctive in the human relationship to language by better understanding what happened with young Keller that day. He explains:

> Here in the well-house in Tuscumbia in a small space and a short time, something extremely important and mysterious had happened. Eight-year-old Helen made her breakthrough from the good responding animal which behaviorists study so successfully to the strange name-giving and sentence-uttering creature who begins by naming shoes and ships and sealing wax, and later tells jokes, curses, reads the paper, writes *La sua volontade e nostra pace,* or becomes a Hegel and composes an entire system of philosophy. [14]

In other words, this new relationship to language transformed Keller's relationship to the world. Words were no longer just tools for communication; they became sources of meaning and understanding. The world changed too; it became a world whose meaning and truth now hinged on the human practice of language.

It is easy to see from this example how empowering such a development is. To the young child who has not yet undergone this kind of transformation, the world is what it is, an ahistorical field of presence. Of course, it is hard for us now as linguistic beings to imagine what life is like without language. Try to imagine for a moment living in a world without any books, newspapers, or websites; without movies and television shows; without private conversations or even any inner monologue.

If you've ever traveled to a place where the language is totally foreign to you, recall how strange this experience can be, and now imagine that, on top of this, you also lacked the ability to reflect on this strangeness through talking, writing, or even any discursive form of thinking. It should be clear that such a transformation would fundamentally alter our relationship to the world we live in. Thus, it is not surprising that, in her description of her breakthrough, Keller writes of a "new sight" that came to her. What she could now "see" was the world coming into "new life" through speech.[15]

Because of her unique situation, Keller underwent this transformation later and more abruptly than most of us. Still, in an important sense, it is something we all undergo. By acquiring language, we come to inhabit a new kind of world—a world that is constantly revitalized (brought into "new life") through speech. As soon as a child starts to learn the names for things, an empowering transformation begins to take place. The child has a frenzied interest early on in learning as many names as possible. We find the same interest evident in Keller's own account when she explains the insight that motivated her newfound eagerness to learn: "Everything had a name, and each name gave birth to a new thought." Recall Percy's description of the world of the human language user which, unlike the nonhuman animal, is a world without gaps. Keller had a basic vocabulary to use before this transformation occurred. What she did not have was a sense for how, with language, the world formed a meaningful totality, nor how, as a participant in that language, she herself would play an active role in articulating that totality. Indeed, Keller now came to understand that the world she had taken for granted, including her inner world, would expand and change as she came to participate in meaningful linguistic activity with others. It was this discovery that so thrilled Keller, making everything "quiver with new life."

Now, few of us will ever have the chance to undergo the kind of experience with language that Keller did. The ontological function of language is, as we have seen, typically neglected in the models by which we commonly understand the world today. Still, in times of crisis we may reconnect with this ontological function. This helps explain the counterintuitive tendency in the modern age for some people to feel more existentially at ease in times of crisis. It helps us to unravel the sort of puzzle that Percy has in mind when he asks: "Why is a man apt to feel bad in a good environment, say suburban Short Hills, New Jersey, on an ordinary Wednesday afternoon? Why is the same man apt to feel good in a very bad environment, say an old hotel on Key Largo during a hurricane?"[16] The answer: in times of crisis, we must exercise our linguistic capacity in order to make sense of things. We have no choice but to become active participants in the interpretation of our lives. As it turns out, this is quite fulfilling.[17] Percy knew this well. He entered medical school as a young man, but after contracting tuberculosis he was forced to take time away from his training to convalesce. During this time, Percy found himself asking questions he never had before. Unable to focus his attention on medicine, he turned to reading philosophy and existentialism in particular. In doing so, he found a new sense of purpose. Percy never returned to medical school. In his own life, then, he had come to understand that the well-being of a person consists not simply of the proper functioning of the human body as an organism, but in the exercise of one's capacity to wonder and to transform one's world through inquiry—that is, in one's capacity as a linguistic being. Thus began Percy's quest to find philosophical treatments of language that could account for this need—a need that he found largely repressed in the modern age.

HEIDEGGER, LANGUAGE, AND WORLD DISCLOSURE

Percy was not the only thinker during the twentieth century to be fascinated with the ontological significance of the human capacity for language and disturbed by how little recognition of this capacity exists today. Both ideas were also essential to the development of phenomenology and, in particular, to hermeneutic phenomenology, which started to emerge in the earlier part of the twentieth century in response to some of the same cultural changes that motivated Percy's own writing. Indeed, as I will suggest here, phenomenology was especially influential on Percy's own analysis of what distinguishes the human capacity for language and why this matters.

Phenomenology first emerged as a philosophical movement early in the twentieth century. It emerged at that time primarily as a critique of certain Enlightenment ideas that, while once radical, had become entrenched dogmas of modern thought. Phenomenologists worried specifically about the modern tendency to attempt to understand the world in isolation of the subject and the subject in isolation of its world—a tendency viewed as complicit in the decline of humanistic inquiry.[18] The idea, still popular today, that good science requires an empiricism purged of any trace of the inquirer is the legacy of this modern tradition. Following in the steps of eighteenth-century philosopher Immanuel Kant, phenomenology rejected pure empiricism as a model of knowing by showing how all experiences necessarily conform to certain laws of subjective experience. What is most certain, phenomenologists claim, is not the object considered independently from consciousness, as empiricists would argue, but the object as it is *for consciousness*.[19] But phenomenology is not simply a subjective affair, exchanging an emphasis on *objects* of experience for an emphasis on the *subject*. For phenomenology, just as raw sense data is an abstraction, so too is the idea of a purely subjective representation. As Edmund Husserl explained it, all consciousness is consciousness *of* something. It is never merely subjective. This is the basis on which the phenomenologist claims, as Husserl did, to go "back to the things themselves."[20] For Husserl's successor, Martin Heidegger, this is paramount. It is by examining the structures of human existence, not setting them aside, that we can best proceed with ontology. And yet inquiry of this kind had become devalued in the modern age. Deprived of its ontological and cognitive import, consciousness had become regarded as merely subjective.

It is in this context that Heidegger produced his major contribution to phenomenology, *Being and Time*. In this work, Heidegger aimed to bring to light several characteristics of human existence typically overlooked by philosophers and scientists alike in the modern age. For example, Heidegger argues that it is the unique characteristic of human existence that our being is, for us, a question. It is not, for us, immediately settled what we are or what we should be. Our existence [*Dasein*] is an issue for us. We can see in this what must have been inspirational for Percy. As he lay in bed, coughing and fatigued from the tuberculosis, on leave from medical school, Percy became a question to himself. Moreover, for Heidegger, like Percy, such crisis situations (while rare) can reveal to us the true nature of our mode of being—the being for whom being is an issue.

Of course, we are not always in such a crisis. For the most part, this characteristic of our existence manifests itself in a very different way, namely, in our tendency to immerse ourselves in a world full of meaning, allowing this meaning to function in our lives tacitly, pre-reflectively as a guide for our thoughts and actions. This is what Heidegger has in mind when he talks about the existential structure of "being-in-the-world" [*In-der-Welt-sein*]. By immersing ourselves in a world of meaning, we act on our fundamental concern for our being. We are not simply indifferent. Immersed in the world of the university as a professor, for example, I act with concern for the well-being of my students and with concern for the campus as a space for learning. I encounter my students as fellow inquirers in the quest for deeper understanding and, unless something happens that requires me to act otherwise, as trustworthy. If, on the other hand, I am immersed as a student in a martial arts class, my cares and concerns are different. Things disclose themselves differently too. My intention in this case is to master the technical skills that I am learning and, if sparring, to avoid submission or injury. Here I encounter my training partners as trustworthy too, but also as competitors. In these ways, the worlds I am immersed in shape not only what I care about, but even shape the basic way in which things appear to me. This is what Heidegger means when he says that to have a world is to have things "show themselves in our concern for the environment."[21]

For Heidegger, then, this is the way in which things show themselves, as he often says, "proximally and for the most part" [*zunächst und zumeist*]. They are disclosed to us not through an act of mental synthesis but in the context of our practical dealings and as meaningful in the context of a particular world or, as Heidegger puts it, as "ready-to-hand" [*zu-handen*].[22] In my examples above, the others I encounter appear to me *as* trustworthy, *as* needy, *as* competitors, and so on, depending on the world in which I encounter them. While the familiar claim of the empiricists, then, is that beings appear as they really are only when we set aside our practical interests, Heidegger argues that beings appear to us, proximally and for the most part, through such pre-reflective acts, and that such appearances constitute "understanding" [*Verstehen*] in its most basic sense.[23]

In claiming that there is understanding at work in the basic ways in which things are disclosed to us, Heidegger is not arguing that I intentionally make a deliberate choice to immerse myself in these ways. Understanding, in Heidegger's sense of the term, is not a voluntary, intentional action. "When we have to do with anything," Heidegger says, "the mere seeing of the Things which are closest to us bears in itself the structure of interpretation."[24] I certainly had choices when it came to being a university professor and practicing martial arts, but I am not consciously making choices about how these different roles and others like them deeply affect my interpretation of things. I find myself thrown into these roles, roles that carry with them implicit ways of interpreting the world. Heidegger uses the term "thrownness" [*Geworfenheit*] to refer to the existential structure whereby one is immersed in a world prior to any choice or reflection.

It is in the context of understanding and interpretation that language first arises as a topic in *Being and Time*. In his exposition on "being-in as such," Heidegger explains that verbal assertions are a mode of interpretation, that is, a way of explicating understanding. Assertions thus derive their sense from the particular ways in which we dwell in the world with others. If I hear someone tell me, "The hammer is too heavy," Heidegger explains that what I discover is not a representation but "an entity in the way that is ready-to-hand."[25] In other words, what is disclosed to me in hearing such speech belongs to the world in which I dwell with others. When I pass my colleague in the hall in late November and she whispers, sighing, "two more weeks," I know that this means she has grown exhausted from the work of the semester and is looking forward to the holiday break. Likewise, if I am grappling with a partner at the gym who gives me two quick taps on the shoulder, I immediately know to stop. Should my colleague have tapped me twice on the shoulder outside of my office, it would be unclear to me what she meant to say. These examples go to show that, when we interpret language—verbal or nonverbal— we do so always in the context of shared worlds of practical concern. Like other worldly things we encounter, such expressions are ready-to-hand.[26]

As Lawrence Hatab points out, Heidegger's point here also holds true for the way we learn language.[27] As young children, we learn language as we learn to dwell in worlds of concern with others, orienting ourselves with others toward different practical tasks. Children learn to say "I love you" as a social ritual that makes up part of the practical activities that they are now learning to take part in. They become accustomed to hearing the phrase in moments of tenderness and to reciprocating with those family members who say it to them. Likewise, they learn to call everything that is above them "sky," so that when they hear the phrase "look up in the sky," they know to look up. Proximally and for the most part, then, words are what Hatab, following Heidegger, calls "indicative concepts," that is, concepts that "point back to factical experience for their realization."[28] Moreover, they are, as Heidegger says, "equiprimordial" with understanding.[29] We become immersed in a world of practical concern as we learn how to communicate with others about things in that world.

It should be clear from these examples, though, that the worlds of practical concern in which we dwell do not exist independently from linguistic practices. Our linguistic practices help to shape the worlds we dwell in. The social ritual of saying "I love you" doesn't just express a naturally given emotion but allows people to participate in a shared world of meaning. The role of language in our lives is thus constitutive, creative. As Charles Taylor argues, "possessing language enables us to relate to things in new ways . . . and to have new emotions, goals, relationships. . . . Language transforms our world, using this last word in a clearly Heidegger-derived sense."[30]

It should not be hard to see, then, given his interests, how Percy would find in Heidegger's *Being and Time* a model for thinking about the peculiar nature of the human being and the special role that language plays in human existence. Indeed, Percy cites Heidegger's discussion of the worldhood of Dasein in *Being and Time* as instructive for his own thinking. "There is Heidegger," Percy writes, "who uses the word '*Dasein*' to describe him, the human creature, a being there. The *Dasein*, moreover, inhabits not only an *Umwelt*, an environment, but a *Welt*, a world."[31] This conceptual distinction thus proves to be extremely helpful to Percy in his quest to understand what is distinctive about the human, that is, how language operates largely behind the scenes of reflection to set forth those worlds of meaning that are so familiar to us.

THE LOSS OF THE CREATURE

Heidegger's analysis in *Being and Time* also helped Percy to better recognize the different attitudes that people take toward the disclosive power of language. At any point, we *could* relate to language as Keller did in these reflections—as a way to bring the world constantly into new life. Often, however, we do not. In his essay, "The Loss of the Creature,"

Percy describes the tendency that we have to stop examining something closely as soon as we find the term that is functionally appropriate for it—that is, as soon as we are able to file it away in whatever inventory is appropriate for that practical, social context. He describes, for instance, a student who walks into biology class to find a set of materials on his desk: a scalpel, a probe, a syringe, and one "specimen of *Squalus acanthias*." Here the student is encouraged to see the creature before him, a dogfish, as the experts see it and only as relevant to the practical task at hand. The name used by experts functions as a means of directing attention to that task. Through this process, though, Percy argues, we lose the creature itself, just as the lexicon of botany can make it so that the tree that we laypeople encounter "loses its proper density and mystery as a concrete existent, and, as merely another specimen of a species, becomes itself nugatory."[32] The point applies not only to objects in nature but to human artifacts as well. Regarding his own writing, Walker Percy himself once remarked that the term "Southern novelist"—a term often used to describe the man behind his work—depressed him, "conjuring up as it does a creature both exotic and familiar and therefore boring, like a yak or a llama in a zoo."[33]

Percy's point is not that we should abandon the use of scientific, technical, or categorical terms. We should, however, be aware of the way that such terms can discourage us from interpreting a thing in new ways or finding new meaning in it. Indeed, whenever we start to explore something—be it a new body of literature, a new tree, or a new place, Percy suggests, we should be prepared to struggle against the tendency to use such terms in a way that restricts all thought to a given practical context. We must not let the designation of Percy's work as "Southern literature" lead us to assume, without further investigation, that its primary purpose is to charm readers with nostalgia and wit, just as we ought not let the identification of a creature as "a specimen of *Squalus acanthias*" reduce the creature to an object whose purpose is to be classified, dissected, and reclassified again for scientific research.

The danger of the ready-to-hand speech into which we are immersed, then, be it "Southern novelist" or *Squalus acanthias*, is that it can rid us of the need for further interpretation and thus thwart the development of further understanding. In his essay, "Naming and Being," Percy explains:

> The symbol "sparrow" is, at first, the means by which a creature is known and affirmed and by which you and I become its co-celebrants. Later, however, the same symbol may serve to conceal the creature until it finally becomes invisible. A sparrow becomes invisible in ordinary life because it disappears behind its symbol. If one sees a movement in a tree and recognizes it and says it is "only a sparrow," one is disposing of the creature through its symbolic formulation.[34]

Percy's concern here is inspired by Heidegger's observation that, although we are that being for whom being is a question, our immersion into world of concern provides us with the ongoing opportunity to flee from this fate. In *Being and Time*, Heidegger makes clear that it is largely through a certain use of language that Dasein attempts this flight. One no longer relates to language in terms of its potential to open up a new world and to give us new ends. Instead, it is leveled down, reduced to what Heidegger calls "idle talk" [*Gerede*].[35] With idle talk, a conversation becomes simply an opportunity to reassert what is already familiar and commonly said. Thus, it is to retreat from the disclosive power of language—not by refraining from speech, but by limiting the power of speech.[36] Speech is taken to be only a means of referring to what is already known, and thus what is known independently of speech. Idle talk, Heidegger explains, "not only releases one from the task of genuine understanding, but develops an undifferentiated kind of intelligibility, for which nothing is closed off any longer."[37]

Heidegger's classic example of a subject matter that often elicits idle talk is death. In talking about death, it is common for people to make gestures recognizing its inevitability, treating it as a most familiar and well-documented event (e.g., "we all know that eventually we will die"). What this obscures, though, is the fact that nobody can simply relate to his own death in just this way—as an event that will occur. When one speaks of death this way, one is indeed attempting to turn death into what is familiar—an event that occurs like other events and that we can accordingly anticipate and prepare for. Thus, in subjecting the topic of death to idle talk, one is attempting to flee precisely from being that creature for whom being is a question. Although the case of death is paradigmatic in many ways, it is not the only subject in connection with which idle talk arises. There is a danger of idle talk whenever we encounter an account that has the potential to challenge the horizons of our understanding. For example, in hearing about some disturbing event taking place in the world—say, state-sanctioned murder in the Philippines—it can be tempting to invoke common ways of minimizing the level of concern that is due, say, by remarking on how commonplace such violence is in the world. This, too, is what Percy has in mind when he speaks about disposing of the subject through its symbolic formation.

Through their craft, writers like Percy work against this leveling, striving to make the world and the language that discloses it to us thought provoking. This is what Heidegger has in mind when he tells us that the writer "experiences his poetic calling as a call to the word as the source, as the bourn of Being."[38] The writer deploys language in a way that allows not only for the discovery of what is ready-to-hand in the world, but also for heightened attunement to the role of language in the development of human understanding. Rather than complete absorption in the disclosive power of language, then, Percy's craft offers an opportunity for us as readers to reflect on and be more deliberate about what it means to be a linguistic being—the *zōon logon echon*.

For both Percy and Heidegger, the stakes of preserving this attunement to language are great indeed. Without it, after all, meaning becomes disconnected from the process of human inquiry, deliberation, and interpretation. The meaning and the ends of our existence become independent of these basic social activities. As a result, the world we live in presents us with fewer and fewer questions. We, too, become less of a question to ourselves and, in turn, less capable of understanding what we as human beings need to flourish. This is the crisis we find ourselves in in the modern age. As Percy puts it, "Man knows he is something more than an organism in an environment. . . . Yet he no longer has the means of understanding the traditional Judeo-Christian teaching that the 'something more' is a soul somehow locked in the organism like a ghost in a machine. What is he then? He has not the faintest idea."[39]

This predicament is even more familiar to us today than it was to Heidegger and Percy. One need only think about the lack of support for rigorous public debate, or for humanities and arts programs in American schools, to know that the problem has worsened in the United States over the past few decades. We now find ourselves, more than ever, lacking any sense for what is distinctive about the human's capacity for language. Yet, this crisis is also an opportunity. After all, it was only in the modern age that Percy could have come to grapple with the mystery of what is distinctive about human language as he did. Likewise, it was the gradual disappearance of humanistic inquiry from science, culminating in the twentieth century, that prompted the development of hermeneutic phenomenology—a development that, as we will see, set the stage for Continental philosophy of language thereafter. Just as Percy's own illness as a young man gave him the occasion to question the source of meaning in his own life, the past century has challenged philosophers in a similar way. In the next chapter, we will look more closely at the treatment of language in hermeneutic phenomenology before moving on to examine later developments in twentieth-century Continental thought.

NOTES

1. In the *Nicomachean Ethics*, Aristotle argues that it is not the capacity for survival or perception that is distinctively human, but the capacity for action in accordance with *logos* (language, speech, reasoning). Aristotle, *The Basic Works of Aristotle*, ed. Richard McKeon (New York: Modern Library, 2001), 1098b.

2. Hannah Arendt, *The Human Condition* (Chicago: University of Chicago Press, 1998), 173–84.

3. Walker Percy, "The Delta Factor," in *The Message in the Bottle: How Queer Man Is, How Queer Language Is, and What One Has to Do with the Other* (New York: Picador, 1975), 14.

4. See, for example, three essays focusing on the Peirce-Percy connection in the recently published volume *Walker Percy, Philosopher*, ed. Leslie Marsh (London: Palgrave Macmillan, 2018): "Percy, Peirce, and Parsifal: Intuition's Farther Shore" by Stephen Utz (21–40); "That Mystery Category 'Fourthness' and Its Relationship to the Work of C. S. Peirce" by Stacey E. Ake (63–88); and "Diamonds in the Rough: The Peirce-Percy Semiotic in *The Second Coming*" by Karey Perkins (89–114).

5. Walker Percy, "The Mystery of Language," in *The Message in the Bottle: How Queer Man Is, How Queer Language Is, and What One Has to Do with the Other* (New York: Picador, 1975), 151.

6. Percy, "The Delta Factor," 13.

7. See Helen E. Longino, *Science as Social Knowledge: Values and Objectivity in Scientific Inquiry* (Princeton, NJ: Princeton University Press, 1990) and Helen E. Longino, *The Fate of Knowledge* (Princeton, NJ: Princeton University Press, 2002).

8. Charles P. Bigger, "Logos and Epiphany: Walker Percy's Theology of Language," in *Critical Essays on Walker Percy*, ed. J. Donald Crowley and Sue Mitchell Crowley (Boston, MA: G. K. Hall and Company, 1989), 56.

9. Rizzolatti and his colleagues at the University of Parma first discovered mirror neurons while studying macaque monkeys. They observed that certain neurons fired when the macaques were observing behavior, just the same as if they were engaged in the behavior directly. Rizzolatti later extended this study of mirror neurons to show their role in human language. Giacomo Rizzolatti and Corrado Sinigaglia, *Mirrors in the Brain: How Our Minds Share Actions and Emotions* (Oxford: Oxford University Press, 2008).

10. Arendt, *The Human Condition*, 176.

11. Walker Percy, "Is a Theory of Man Possible?," in *Signposts in a Strange Land* (New York: Picador, 1991), 119.

12. Walker Percy, "The Fateful Rift: The San Andreas Fault in the Human Mind," in *Signposts in a Strange Land* (New York: Picador, 1991), 289.

13. Quoted in Percy, "The Delta Factor," 35.

14. Ibid.

15. Keller was insistent on using metaphors of vision and rejected the idea that they were inaccessible to the blind. In *The World I Live In*, she responds to the policy of the *Matilda Ziegler Magazine for the Blind* to omit stories and poems that allude to visually stunning scenes that would, according to the magazine, only "serve to emphasize the blind man's sense of his affliction." Keller responds: "That is to say, I may not talk about beautiful mansions and gardens because I am poor. I may not read about Paris and the West Indies because I cannot visit them in territorial reality. I may not dream of heaven because it is possible that I may never go there. Yet a venturesome spirit impels me to use words of sight and sound whose meaning I can guess only from analogy and fancy. This hazardous game is half the delight, the frolic, of daily life. I glow as I read of splendors which the eye alone can survey." Helen Keller, "The World I Live In," in *Helen Keller: Selected Writings*, ed. Kim E. Nielsen (New York: New York University Press, 2005), 32.

16. Percy, "The Delta Factor," 4.

17. For a discussion of this theme in Percy's novel *The Thanatos Syndrome*, see Micah Mattix, "Walker Percy's Alternative to Reductive Scientism in *The Thanatos Syndrome*," *Perspectives on Political Science* 40, no. 3 (2011): 147–52.

18. Edmund Husserl, *The Crisis of the European Sciences and Transcendental Phenomenology: An Introduction to Phenomenological Philosophy*, trans. David Carr (Evanston, IL: Northwestern University Press, 1970).

19. It was G. W. F. Hegel who first introduced this argument that twentieth-century phenomenologists later retrieved. See G. W. F. Hegel, *Phenomenology of Spirit*, trans. A. V. Miller (Oxford: Oxford University Press, 1977), 53.

20. Edmund Husserl, *Logical Investigations, Volume 2*, ed. Dermot Moran (London: Routledge, 2001), 168.

21. Martin Heidegger, *Being and Time*, trans. John Macquarrie and Edward Robinson (New York: Harper & Row, 1962), 95.

22. Despite the point of convergence between Heidegger and Husserl discussed above, it should be noted that this claim that things are given to us, first and foremost, through our practical dealings and not through an act of mental synthesis differentiates Heideggerean from Husserlian phenomenology. For a discussion of this point, see Hubert L. Dreyfus, *Being-in-the-World: A Commentary on Heidegger's Being and Time, Division I* (Cambridge, MA: MIT Press, 1992).

23. Heidegger, *Being and Time*, 188. The matter of how to assess the adequacy of understanding in this sense is an ongoing subject of debate. Gilbert Ryle, for example, argues that, although this familiarity with things comes first in the order of knowing, it does not have logical priority, because it is not necessarily valid and could turn out to be false. See Gilbert Ryle, "Heidegger's *Sein und Zeit*," in *Heidegger and Modern Philosophy*, ed. Michael Murray (New Haven, CT: Yale University Press, 1978), 59. Ryle presents this as a point of disagreement with Heidegger, but, as Dreyfus explains, Heidegger does not present this kind of understanding, which Dreyfus calls our "pre-ontological understanding of being," as the complete and final picture of knowledge. See Dreyfus, *Being-in-the-World*, 19–21. As will become clear beginning in the next chapter, it becomes increasingly important for certain figures in the Continental tradition to articulate what must supplement this pre-reflective understanding in order for it to be complete.

24. Heidegger, *Being and Time*, 190.

25. Ibid., 196.

26. Ibid., 204.

27. Lawrence J. Hatab, *Proto-Phenomenology and the Nature of Language: Dwelling in Speech, Volume 1* (London: Rowman & Littlefield International, 2017).

28. Hatab, *Proto-Phenomenology and the Nature of Language*, 15.

29. Heidegger, *Being and Time*, 203.

30. Charles Taylor, *The Language Animal: The Full Shape of the Human Linguistic Capacity* (Cambridge, MA: The Belknap Press of Harvard University Press, 2016), 37.

31. Percy, "The Fateful Rift," 289–90.

32. Walker Percy, "Metaphor as Mistake," in *The Message in the Bottle : How Queer Man Is, How Queer Language Is, and What One Has to Do with the Other* (New York: Picador, 1975), 63.

33. Walker Percy, "Novel Writing in an Apocalyptic Time," in *Signposts in a Strange Land* (New York: Picador, 1991), 153.

34. Walker Percy, "Naming and Being," in *Signposts in a Strange Land* (New York: Picador, 1991), 135.

35. Heidegger, *Being and Time*, 211–14.

36. Andrew Inkpin argues that Heidegger has a deep ambivalence about language in *Being and Time*: "While recognizing its constitutive role in everyday understanding of the world, [in his discussion of *Gerede*] he also clearly insinuates that the understanding it constitutes lacks something important." Andrew Inkpin, *Disclosing the World: On the Phenomenology of Language* (Cambridge, MA: MIT Press, 2016), 70. I am arguing here, however, that for Heidegger, while our immersion into language establishes the danger of idle talk, the two are distinct in one important sense. Our immersion into language is the condition for the pursuit of understanding, while idle talk impedes the development of this understanding.

37. Heidegger, *Being and Time*, 213.

38. Martin Heidegger, "The Nature of Language," in *On the Way to Language*, trans. Peter Hertz (New York: Harper & Row, 1971), 66.

39. Percy, "The Delta Factor," 9.

TWO

Words Underway

Guiding Insights from Hermeneutic Phenomenology

Heidegger's *Being and Time* was groundbreaking in shedding light on the way we dwell in the world and the features of that world issuing from this way of dwelling. As we saw in the previous chapter, it is in this context that Heidegger takes up the topic of language in *Being and Time*. Proximally and for the most part, we interpret the words we hear in the context of some world of practical concern in which we are immersed. It is in such a context that words, for the most part, have their sense. This point helps support Heidegger's argument that human existence has the character of *being-in-the-world*. On Heidegger's own admission, though, the topic of language remained in the background of his philosophical writings until his 1934 lecture series, which focused on the topic of logic and the concept of *logos* (from which the German *Logik* and the English "logic" derive).[1] It is only at this point that Heidegger began to make an exploration of language central to his work. Later he would explain that "because reflection on language, and on Being, has determined my path of thinking from early on, therefore their discussion has stayed as far as possible in the background."[2] In other words, language had been so fundamental to Heidegger in his early thinking, serving as a background to his early investigations, that it did not come into focus as a primary object of investigation itself.

By contrast, language is a central theme in Heidegger's later work. Yet, even in the later work, his primary interest is in formulating and thinking through the problem of how to properly engage and understand language. This is nowhere clearer than in the lectures and essays from the 1950s collected in the volume *On the Way to Language*, which emphasize language's non-immediacy and hence, as the title suggests, the need to make *a way to* language. At the beginning of "The Way to Language," for example, Heidegger argues that, because we have the ability to speak—indeed, because we are constantly immersed in language—we tend not to see a need for a transformation in our relationship to language.

> We are, then, within language and with language before all else. A way to language is not needed. Besides, the way to language is impossible if we indeed are already at that point to which the way is to take us. But are we at that point? Are we so fully within language that we experience its nature, that we think speech as speech by grasping its idiom in listening to it? Do we in fact already live close to language even without our doing? Or is the way to language as language the longest road our thinking can follow?[3]

But what does it mean to speak about a "way to language," and why is this undertaking the "longest road our thinking can follow"? Surely, after all, the point is not to withdraw one of the most significant arguments of *Being and Time*, namely, that Dasein has a pre-reflective understanding of the world and, by extension, of the language into which it is thrown. How is it, then, that one can stay true to this phenomenological insight while also arguing that language is somehow non-immediate for us? In order to answer this question, I focus in this chapter on Heidegger's *On the Way to Language*, his most mature and focused treatment on the topic of language. I argue that Heidegger's later work is helpful in bringing to light some of the ways in which language can appear to us as non-immediate, but that his analysis of this non-immediacy becomes problematic when presented as an absolute rather than as a moment in a larger development. I then argue that a better way of making sense of language's non-immediacy is to be found in the work of Hans-Georg Gadamer, Heidegger's student and lifelong interlocutor, for whom the non-immediacy of language is but a moment in the larger process of understanding.

NON-IMMEDIACY IN *ON THE WAY TO LANGUAGE*

The writings collected in *On the Way to Language* make clear that during this period Heidegger had been struck with the mystery of language. Like Percy, he was struck by how philosophers of language and linguists were generally overlooking essential aspects of language. Moreover, he had become fascinated with those cases in which we experience language as conspicuously *unready-to-hand*, as happens, for example, "when we cannot find the right word for something that concerns us, carries us away, oppresses or encourages us," and with the prospect of rethinking language on the basis of such cases.[4] As indicated above, all of this marks a shift from Heidegger's treatment of language in *Being and Time*, in which understanding was presented as equiprimordial with language.[5]

The emphasis here was on the tacit understanding that we have of language—an understanding that we start to acquire from early childhood and that becomes second nature to us. In his later work, Heidegger retains the argument that our primary relationship to language is immersive in this way but places a new emphasis on the need to "make our way to language."[6]

For example, in "The Nature of Language," a set of lectures delivered in Freiburg in 1957 and 1958, Heidegger urges us to consider a certain ambivalence that characterizes our relationship to language. For the most part, he explains, we relate to language as something that we are always speaking, something we are always engaged with as a tacit mode of understanding. "Even so," he says, "our relation to language is vague, obscure, almost speechless."[7] This description is consistent with Heidegger's characterization of human language in *Being and Time* as pre-reflective, as equiprimordial with the understanding with which Dasein inhabits the world. Here, however, Heidegger's remarks—indeed the lectures as a whole—are intended to provoke a transformation in our relationship to language. They are intended, as Heidegger himself puts it, to "bring us face to face with a possibility of undergoing an experience with language," that is, of undergoing something transformative with language that befalls us and is not of our own making.[8] A year later, in a lecture titled "The Way to Language" delivered in Berlin, Heidegger again tells us that the intent of his lecture is to bring language into new light and thus transform our relation to it. In both lectures, then, Heidegger suggests that the tacit, given understanding that we have of the language we speak is not the only way that we can relate to language. We may, instead, become struck by the language we encounter in a way that opens up something new about language. Moreover, in order to prepare for such experiences, we may "rid ourselves of the habit of always hearing only what we already understand"[9] and in this way come to encounter language in its non-immediacy.

It is this kind of encounter with language that takes place in "A Dialogue on Language," another piece included in *On the Way to Language*. The dialogue is a somewhat fictitious reconstruction of Heidegger's conversation with the Japanese scholar and professor of German literature Tomio Tezuka, who visited Heidegger in Freiburg in 1954.[10] In the dialogue, the two discuss the difficulty of properly grasping the essence of language. Early in their conversation, they suggest that the understanding one has of language from the everyday, pragmatic use of the term is not in itself adequate for grasping this essence, since in hearing the term "language" it is easy to assume that what is to be thought is something already familiar and easily grasped. It is thus easy to ignore what, say, the Western concept of language leaves "unthought." Thus, they reason, if one really wants to understand the essence of language, one must forge a path—a *way*—to it, and this will naturally involve an attempt to reorient the way that one listens to language.

For Heidegger, then, there is something to be gained by listening differently. But how, more positively, should we listen? In "A Dialogue on Language," Heidegger suggests that we must learn to hear words we encounter as "hints."[11] A hint, Heidegger tells us elsewhere, "lets us only suspect at first the memorable thing toward which it beckons us, as a thought-worthy matter for which the fitting mode of thinking is still lacking."[12] A hint, then, is something indicative that holds what it discloses partially in suspense, making it more thought worthy. But what does it mean to listen to language as a hint in this sense? After all, the description surely sounds strange to us today in an age when we tend to take computer language as a model for all language. With such a model, we tend to see language as a set of rules that, if followed, allow a person to produce in another an intended representation or response, just as a programming language allows us to communicate instructions to a machine. Given this, it can be difficult to make sense of Heidegger's claim that language, in its essence, speaks like a hint or a gesture. When asked by the inquirer about whether there is in Japanese a word for "language," however, it is precisely this description of language as a hint and a gesture that eventually "emboldens" the Japanese character to offer a response. The response is not simply an attempt at finding that word that signifies the same thing or that is used in an identical set of practical contexts. It is "*Koto ba*," an old Japanese word that the speaker gradually translates for the inquirer as the conversation unfolds. "Language, heard through this word," he explains, "is: the petals that stem from *Koto*," that is, from the "happening of the lightening message of the graciousness that brings forth."[13] As the interpretation unfolds, the inquirer exclaims that the term appears indeed to be a "wondrous word, and therefore inexhaustible to our thinking."[14] What the dialogue appears to praise, then, is a kind of listening that takes speaking as a hint and a kind of speaking that opens up something inexhaustible for thought.

This point requires some clarification, though. After all, it might seem that such a concept of language does nothing more than to turn language into the very opposite of what we normally take it to be. Instead of making something clear to our thinking, it confounds our thinking and presents us with something whose meaning is inexhaustible and indeterminate. Instead of language being equiprimordial with understanding, language is now presented as defying our attempt to understand.[15] Some of Heidegger's own formulations, in fact, give rise to such concerns. In "The Nature of Language," for example, Heidegger argues that "the essential nature of language flatly refuses to express itself in words—in the language, that is, in which we make statements about language."[16] Likewise, "The Way to Language" begins by invoking a line from Novalis that reads: "The peculiar property of language, namely that language is concerned exclusively with itself—precisely that is known to no one."[17] At such moments, it seems as though the non-immediacy of language rests in the fact that it is impenetrable to understanding. Moreover, the non-immediate quality of language seems to be presented here as the true nature of language, a nature that is hidden from us for the most part but occasionally can be grasped. While these formulations do indeed raise such concerns, I will suggest here that a better way of understanding the claim that language is a hint is in terms of the unique kind of understanding that is called for by non-immediate language. It is Heidegger's student, Hans-Georg Gadamer, who develops this point most clearly.

GADAMER ON NON-IMMEDIACY AS A MOMENT OF RECOGNITIVE UNDERSTANDING

Hermeneutics as a discipline first arose during the nineteenth century at a time when many scholars of literature, broadly speaking, were starting to see their own perspectives as historically situated. Scholars of law, biblical scripture, and ancient literature, for example, had begun to worry about the historical distance between the time in which the texts they studied were first composed and the time in which they were now being read. These texts, after all, were written by people whose lives were very different from the lives of contemporary readers. Hermeneutics initially arose, then, in a context where the non-immediacy of language was taken to be a problem. It offered a way of investigating what understanding ought to mean in such contexts and, practically speaking, what specific methods of interpretation it ought to entail.

For many theorists of hermeneutics, the solution to the problem involves reconstructing, as much as possible, the historical and linguistic conditions in which the authors of the texts lived, or the thought processes of the authors themselves. This was the approach of Friedrich Schleiermacher, widely considered the founder of modern hermeneutics.[18] Gadamer's own contribution to hermeneutic philosophy went in a very different direction, however. Like his nineteenth-century hermeneutic predecessors, Gadamer was likewise interested in making sense of the kind of understanding that can take place in encounters with an object whose meaning is not immediately available. Instead of seeing such objects as merely problematic and as sources of frustration, though, Gadamer takes them as serving a positive role in the development of understanding.

We can begin to understand Gadamer's point if we consider the experience of art, a topic that Gadamer explored extensively throughout his career. When we encounter an artwork, we know that the meaning is not what is given to us immediately. What strikes us first of all about the artwork is that it presents us with an interpretive challenge. The work makes a claim on us in this way. This is especially true of those works that we recognize as originating in a time, place, and set of circumstances significantly different from our own. In encountering a work of art, we ask ourselves: What is it saying? We interpret it. But the task of interpretation here is not, for Gadamer, the task of reconstruction outlined by Schleiermacher. It is not a matter of setting oneself and one's own time aside to grasp what the artist originally intended or what the piece once meant to its original audience. The performing arts makes this especially clear. Whenever a work is performed, staged, or exhibited, the work cannot be presented exactly as it was originally performed, staged, or exhibited. To ask what the work says is to ask what it says to us today.

But interpretation here is not the foisting of subjective associations onto the work. Each audience views the work from its own horizon, but what it takes away is not merely the imprint of its own subjectivity. To find out what the artwork says to us in the present time, we must allow the work to interrogate us. This means coming to see some of the habitual presuppositions that we carry as particular and finite, thus allowing our understanding to expand beyond the limits of our present presuppositions. Interpretation involves, then, a bidirectional movement: not only the movement of rendering the unfamiliar object familiar, but also the movement by which the familiar becomes unfamiliar. As Gadamer puts it in "Aesthetics and Hermeneutics," "The intimacy with which the work of art touches us is at the same time, in enigmatic fashion, a shattering and a demolition of the familiar. It is not only the 'This art thou!' disclosed in a joyous and frightening shock; it also says to us; 'Thou must alter thy life!'"[19]

If we were to think about the process of understanding simply as the registering of something immediate (say, in the way that an electronic personal assistant "understands" your voice), then this bidirectional movement of disclosure would have no place in the process. But understanding clearly involves more than the registering of something immediate. Yes, we use the word "understanding" in this way, as when, for example, I tell the nurse that I do not understand the first question on the form he gave me. We also, however, use the term to refer to something that we develop cumulatively over time, as when we speak about the understanding that the experienced nurse possesses. It is understanding in this sense that we actively seek out throughout our lives. And it is this sense of understanding that we take pleasure in because, unlike the first type, it involves the full use of our cognitive faculties.

Such understanding is not entirely separate from the first type, however. Rather, it is a matter of enriching and deepening immediate understanding, of deepening how we know what we are pre-reflectively familiar with; this is why Gadamer describes this understanding as an act of "recognition."[20] It is recognitive understanding that results from interpretation, which is to say, from our encounters with those objects whose meanings are not immediate. Through the bidirectional movement of interpretation, we make use of our given, pre-reflective understanding to render something unfamiliar familiar, but at the same time, what is familiar comes to be known in a new light. A part of our pre-reflective understanding is brought to light for us and is raised to greater truth. This can only happen, though, in cases where meaning is not immediate. Thus, rather than treating the non-immediacy of art as a deficiency, Gadamer suggests that philosophical hermeneutics ought to recognize the unique cognitive import of such encounters. Art helps to deepen, enrich, and transform our knowledge of the world, and it is on account of this—its cognitive import—that humans are drawn to art. Art deepens our understanding of the world with which we are already familiar.

The same can be said for that other famous object of non-immediacy, the text. Texts are, for Gadamer, the most non-immediate. "Nothing is so strange, and at the same time so demanding, as the written word," he writes in *Truth and Method*.[21] A text comes to us as if redacted of any connection to the time, place, and circumstances in which it arose. When all we have is the text, we do not have the author present before us who can be questioned or who can clarify the intended meaning.[22] Nor are we ourselves immersed in the world in which that author wrote. What a text demands, though, is not the reconstruction of this lost world, nor, unless I am a historian of ideas, a forensic investigator, or a censor, that I try to "get inside another person and relive his experiences."[23] But this is not to say that there is simply no way of understanding a text. The understanding required is, rather, bidirectional and recognitive, just as the interpretation of art is. In reading a written document—be it religious scripture, a legal document, or an ancient treatise, I make it contemporaneous to me. I figure out what it says now, that is, what is says to us today. My reading makes the past present in this way. I am participating in a process of understanding, of interpretation. But to read is not simply to turn the text into a mirror so that one finds in it only what we already knew. As with art, the interpretation of a text gives us the chance to reflect on, to enrich, and to deepen our understanding of what is already familiar to us. As I read a text, I find that the subject matter has not been exhausted by what I have read, that there is more that must be said about it. In this sense, the text appears to me to be a "living" text. It belongs, we might say, to the living life of language, that is, the evolution of language as it continually calls for and reflects the development of conscious thought. In this way, the words that I read can be said to provide a "hint." They bring forth a subject matter and, in so doing, reveal things about it; however, they do so in a way that demands further understanding.[24]

What comes out of the interaction between the reader and the text, then, is more than either the intention of the author or the preconceptions of the reader. For example, if I am reading an ancient treatise on virtue, I

inevitably understand the subject matter of the treatise through a lens
that is familiar to me, say, through concepts and stories with which I am
already familiar; in doing so, however, these preconceptions are themselves put at risk. As Gadamer argues, "the interpreter's own horizon is
decisive, yet not as a personal standpoint that he maintains or enforces,
but more as an opinion and a possibility that one brings into play and
puts at risk, and that helps one truly make one's own what the text
says."[25]

The kind of understanding required from a text is made especially
clear when we consider the case of translation, for example, when reading a text in a foreign language. Because there is no one-to-one correspon-
dence between languages, the reader in this case cannot hope to simply
render the text word-for-word into the new language without giving any
thought to the subject matter itself. The task of the translator, Gadamer
explains, is not to produce a copy but to place herself "in the direction of
what is said (i.e., in its meaning) in order to carry over what is to be said
into the direction of [her] own saying."[26] It is, in other words, to recognize and to re-present the meaning of what has been said, raising it to its
truth.

As we can see, then, for Gadamer, encounters with the non-immediate
play a positive role in the development of understanding. When I encounter something whose meaning is immediate, there is no reason for
me to expand my current worldview or revise the concepts that I use to
make sense of the world. By contrast, when I am confronted with an
object that is in some way unfamiliar to me—like an artwork or a text—I
am forced to be more reflective about the presuppositions that I carry
with me and that I use habitually to make sense of things. Hence, for
Gadamer, while historical texts lack the immediacy of other historical
artifacts, their lack is not a defect; rather, Gadamer claims, "this apparent
lack, the abstract alienness of all 'texts,' uniquely expresses the fact that
everything in language belongs to the process of understanding."[27]

HERMENEUTICAL ACTIVITY IN *ON THE WAY TO LANGUAGE*

In light of Gadamer's argument, let us return to Heidegger's point that
the essential power of a word is to offer a hint or a gesture. It should now
be clear that Gadamer's discussion of non-immediate language sheds
light on this description and that it does so by explaining the importance
of the understanding we develop in interaction with non-immediate language. With a lot of the language we hear, what is meant is immediately
clear to us and requires no reflection. With non-immediate language,
though, it is different. Non-immediate language speaks by soliciting us to
interpret the subject matter brought forward and thus to participate in
the cumulative process by which it is understood. When it speaks, "it

does not simply speak its word, always the same, in lifeless rigidity, but gives ever new answers to the person who questions it and poses ever new questions to him who answers it."[28] It is this quality of language, the living life of language, that makes it appear so that a text gives its readers only hints. For the meaning of the text, what is says, can only be found in the interaction between the text and its readers.

For Gadamer, then, the point is not to think about language as that which defies intelligibility and thwarts our attempts to understand it. Heidegger himself, however, is not always so clear on this point. In the interest of accenting the strange, non-immediate character of certain concepts and texts passed down to us from the past, and in disabusing us of the tendency to restrict language to a purely instrumental function, his formulations in his later work sometimes misconstrue the basis for the mystery of language. Indeed, Heidegger often speaks about language as though it were something always and absolutely non-immediate, overlooking the fact that non-immediacy is but a moment in the process of human understanding.

Yet Heidegger's account appears more consistent with Gadamer's if we look not just to what he says but also to what he *does* in his lectures, that is, to their performative dimension. For Gadamer, after all, understanding comes about when one engages in that bidirectional movement of interpretation. Looking, then, to the way Heidegger engages in interpretation in the lectures, we can better take stock of where Heidegger's philosophy of language is consistent with, and perhaps even indebted to, Gadamer.

For example, consider again "A Dialogue on Language," the fictitious dialogue that Heidegger wrote on the occasion of Tomio Tezuka's visit to Freiburg. While language becomes the subject matter at one point in the conversation between the two characters, the conversation is not simply about language but also a way of enacting language and letting its ontological force appear. This is why, as Graham Parkes points out, Heidegger's title describes a dialogue taking place not just about (*über*) language but from (*von*) language.[29] In it, we see not only a conversation about language but the enacting of language in the form of a dialogue. The dialogue represents, in fact, what Heidegger himself hoped to do with the scholars from Japan who had been coming to Germany to study with or collaborate with him, scholars like Tezuka, Seinosuke Yuasa, and Shin'ichi Hisamatsu. Heidegger was quite interested in Japanese culture and the Japanese intellectual tradition but, even with a steady stream of guest scholars from Japan, proceeded with extreme caution in his attempt to understand this tradition that he found so markedly different from Western metaphysics.[30] He clearly did not wish to rush into an interpretation of the Japanese philosophical tradition and thus to lose out on the possibility of transforming his understanding through the encounter. So, he sought dialogues with his guests and showed particular interest in the interpretation of Japanese language.[31]

In "A Dialogue on Language," the subject matter of language arises when the inquirer, now clearly Heidegger, is asked about the role of hermeneutics in his early work and about the prominent role of language in his recent thought. After describing what has interested him on the topic of language, Heidegger asks his interlocutor whether there is a word for *Sprache* in Japanese and about how language is experienced in the Japanese world. He asks, in other words, for a thoughtful translation of the word. Now, it might seem that, given Heidegger's general hesitation, he would resist any attempt at translation so as not to level away the strangeness and non-immediacy of language. The two interlocutors do not simply conclude that the task is futile, though. At the same time, they do not rush to find a word in the Japanese language that is used in the same way that *Sprache* is used. Rather, they take the challenge as an opportunity to bring into play and to interrogate their own linguistic and cultural horizons and, through this mutual interrogation, to develop a new, shared understanding of their subject matter. What results through the discussion of *Koto ba* is, for both interlocutors, a deeper understanding of the nature of language.[32] This is an understanding that develops as both speakers try to articulate what they already know to the other, and try to integrate what they learn from the other into what they know. The process of understanding that takes place in "A Dialogue on Language" is, then, recognitive and cumulative in just the way that Gadamer describes.

Although conversation is particularly generative of this kind of understanding, it should not be surprising, based on what Gadamer has said, to see the same process at work in Heidegger's interpretation of texts. For Gadamer, after all, "to understand a text is to come to understand oneself in a kind of dialogue."[33] *On the Way to Language* includes three lectures structured around an interpretation of a poem: "The Nature of Language," "Words," and "Language in the Poem." In each of these lectures, Heidegger demonstrates the point that listening to language requires undertaking the task of interpretation. As he reads poems by Friedrich Hölderlin, Georg Trakl, and Stefan George, he is careful to look out for what is "strange" in the thoughts that the poems bring forth, that is, for what challenges the very preconceptions that he necessarily brings with him as a reader. This is why he draws so much attention in his readings of the poems to what withholds itself from immediate understanding. In his reading of a poem from George, for example, he is careful to search out what in the poem resists an immediate rendering of its meaning. Of the poem's last stanza, for example, Heidegger insists that "we must be careful not to force the vibration of the poetic saying into the rigid groove of a univocal statement, and so destroy it."[34] Such words of caution, however, do not put the brakes on the task of interpretation. Heidegger still proceeds with interpreting George's poem. Indeed, "the vibration of the poetic saying" is precisely what makes such a claim on Heidegger, compelling him to proceed with consistent attention to the poem. Thus, in his interpretation of poetry, just like in his engagement with translation, we see Heidegger taking the non-immediacy of language as a moment in the process of understanding.

This development in hermeneutic phenomenology ought to be instructive for us. After all, it is easy for philosophers of language to neglect the importance of non-immediacy in the phenomenon that we study. It is easy to focus exclusively on how the sense of words is bound to the worldly objects that they reference or to the practical social tasks that the words help us to perform. As we have seen, this was Heidegger's concern in his early work. Early on, Heidegger too emphasized the way that our understanding of language reflects our pre-reflective familiarity with the world, the way that when we hear a phrase, we understand immediately what is being said. Given such an emphasis on language as pre-reflective understanding, then, it is not hard to see why such analyses had so little to say about language that makes a claim on us, demands interpretation from us, and even transforms what we understand.

As we have seen in this chapter, however, by the middle of the twentieth century, there were important voices in the Continental tradition that had begun to take seriously the positive role in understanding played by the non-immediacy of language. For Gadamer, we run into non-immediate language when the words we encounter require us to pause, to revise some of our presuppositions, and to theorize about the subject matter from this revised perspective. Rather than treating non-immediacy simply as an obstacle for understanding, though, Gadamer sees it as pivotal for its development. Moreover, for Gadamer, non-immediate language is something we encounter every day. It is not exceptionally rare. We find it wherever there is meaningful conversation with another—be it a live interlocutor or the author of a text, where the conversation leads us to see things differently. It is this hermeneutic account, I argue, that best enables us to make sense of Heidegger's call for a way to language. What's more, as we will see in the next two chapters, it is this hermeneutic account of language that has enabled Continental philosophers in recent decades to better understand the importance in our lives of speaking and writing and, on the other hand, of being heard. In the next chapter, I look more specifically at how this insight developed as Continental philosophers began to grapple with a literature rife with non-immediacy—the literature produced by survivors of the Holocaust.

NOTES

1. The text of the lecture has been reconstructed on the basis of student transcripts. See Martin Heidegger, *Logic as the Question Concerning the Essence of Language*, trans. Wanda Torres Gregory and Yvonne Unna (Albany: State University of New York Press, 2009).

2. Martin Heidegger, "A Dialogue on Language," in *On the Way to Language*, trans. Peter D. Hertz (New York: Harper & Row, 1971), 7.

3. Martin Heidegger, "The Way to Language," in *On the Way to Language*, trans. Peter D. Hertz (New York: Harper & Row, 1971), 112.

4. Martin Heidegger, "The Nature of Language," in *On the Way to Language*, trans. Peter D. Hertz (New York: Harper & Row, 1971), 59.

5. Martin Heidegger, *Being and Time*, trans. John Macquarrie and Edward Robinson (New York: Harper & Row, 1962), 203.

6. Dennis Schmidt describes Heidegger's later caution about language as a caution against "presuming that such an experience is readily available, or even that we might know the original form of such an experience." Schmidt goes on to point out that this caution leads Heidegger to an increased interest in poetry and translation as his career develops, because in these forms "the word itself is put into question." Dennis Schmidt, *Lyrical and Ethical Subjects: Essays on the Periphery of the Word, Freedom, and History* (Albany: State University of New York Press, 2005), 104.

7. Heidegger, "The Nature of Language," 58.

8. Ibid., 57.

9. Ibid., 58.

10. One can compare Heidegger's creative reconstruction with Tezuka's own account of the conversation, provided in Reinhard May, "Tezuka Tomio, 'An Hour with Heidegger,'" in *Heidegger's Hidden Sources: East Asian Influences on His Work*, trans. Graham Parkes (London: Routledge, 1996), 59–64.

11. Heidegger, "A Dialogue on Language," 24–27.

12. Heidegger, "The Nature of Language," 96.

13. Heidegger, "A Dialogue on Language," 47.

14. Ibid., 47.

15. Karen S. Feldman argues that Heidegger's own use of language in *Being and Time* is an attempt to use language to reveal the limits of language. In particular, Feldman argues that *Being and Time* is not a discussion of being but a performance of language's inability to represent being. She observes that, in Heidegger's book, "the very words of the investigation into being are wrested out of readiness-to-hand, in part by devices such as italics, scare quotes, hyphenation, invention, and etymology, which thematize or make conspicuous the word-character of the words." Karen S. Feldman, *Binding Words: Conscience and Rhetoric in Hobbes, Hegel, and Heidegger* (Evanston, IL: Northwestern University Press, 2006), 88.

16. Heidegger, "The Nature of Language," 81.

17. Heidegger, "The Way to Language," 111.

18. Friedrich Schleiermacher, *Hermeneutics and Criticism* (Cambridge: Cambridge University Press, 1998).

19. Hans-Georg Gadamer, "Aesthetics and Hermeneutics," in *Philosophical Hermeneutics*, trans. David E. Linge (Berkeley: University of California Press, 1977), 104. Gadamer's remarks here make clear that, contrary to Derrida's criticism, he indeed understands the "interruption of rapport" to be a condition for understanding. For Derrida's criticism, see Jacques Derrida, "Three Questions for Gadamer," in *Dialogue and Deconstruction: The Gadamer-Derrida Encounter*, ed. Diane P. Michelfelder and Richard E. Palmer (Albany: State University of New York Press, 1989), 53.

20. In the section of *Truth and Method* titled "The Ontology of the Work of Art," Gadamer argues that the pleasure that human beings take in art comes from the pleasure we find in those imitations that allow for recognition. "But we do not understand what recognition is in its profoundest nature if we only regard it as knowing

something again that we know already—i.e., what is familiar is recognized again. The joy of recognition," Gadamer explains, "is rather the joy of knowing more than is already familiar. In recognition what we know emerges, as if illuminated, from all the contingent and variable circumstances that condition it; it is grasped in its essence." Hans-Georg Gadamer, *Truth and Method*, trans. Joel Weinsheimer and Donald G. Marshall (London: Bloomsbury, 2004), 118.

21. Gadamer, *Truth and Method*, 163.

22. Walter Ong's research into oral cultures reveals how this situation tended to provoke anxiety in people first introduced to writing. Walter Ong, *Orality and Literacy* (London: Routledge, 2012). Perhaps the most well-known example of such anxiety appears in Plato's *Phaedrus*, in which Socrates expresses concerns about the effect that the invention of writing will have on human memory and understanding. See *Plato: Complete Works*, ed. John M. Cooper (Indianapolis, IN: Hackett, 1997), 274b–276a.

23. Gadamer, *Truth and Method*, 402.

24. In their frequent demand for interpretation, texts clearly differ from ordinary indicative language. However, as James Risser has argued, this should not lead us to assume that all spoken language lacks the ideality of the text. My treatment of the hermeneutical activity of dialogue in the next section, I hope, will help to illustrate this point. See James Risser, *Hermeneutics and the Voice of the Other: Re-reading Gadamer's Philosophical Hermeneutics* (Albany: State University of New York Press, 1997).

25. Gadamer, *Truth and Method*, 406.

26. Hans-Georg Gadamer, "Man and Language," in *Philosophical Hermeneutics*, trans. David E. Linge (Berkeley: University of California Press, 1977), 68.

27. Gadamer, *Truth and Method*, 407.

28. Hans-Georg Gadamer, "On the Problem of Self-Understanding," in *Philosophical Hermeneutics*, trans. David E. Linge (Berkeley: University of California Press, 1977), 57. One thinks here also of Helen Keller's reflection on what it takes to become a writer. "You see, there is but one road to authorship," Keller writes. "It remains for ever a way in which each man must go a-pioneering. . . . What I mean is, we can follow where literary folk have gone; but, in order to be authors ourselves, to be followed, we must strike into a path where no one has preceded us." Helen Keller, *Out of the Dark* (London: Hodder and Stoughton, 1913), 120.

29. Graham Parkes, "Afterwords Language," in *Heidegger and Asian Thought*, ed. Graham Parkes (Honolulu: University of Hawaii Press, 1987), 213.

30. This caution is also apparent in the conversation that Heidegger has with Hisamatsu about art, a conversation that proceeds—like in "A Dialogue on Language"—by thinking through the differences between "Eastern" and "Western" conceptions of art. See Martin Heidegger, Hoseki Shin'ichi Hisamatsu, Alfred L. Copley, et al., "Art and Thinking: Protocol of a Colloquium on May 18, 1958," trans. Carolyn Culbertson and Tobias Keiling, *Philosophy Today* 61, no. 1 (2017): 47–51.

31. In his interactions with his guests from Japan, the topic of language was naturally important, since several of the guests were involved in the translation of Heidegger's works into Japanese. Heidegger's attention to this particular language, then, reflects his interest in these translation projects. It is worth recalling too that Heidegger's work was first translated into Japanese in 1930, 19 years before any translation was published in English.

32. According to his own report, Tezuka also regarded the conversation as a mutually enriching one. See May, "Tezuka Tomio, 'An Hour with Heidegger,'" 59–64.

33. Gadamer, "On the Problem of Self-Understanding," 57.

34. Heidegger, "The Nature of Language," 64.

THREE

On Linguistic Trauma and the Demand to Write

Continental Philosophy and the Literature of the Holocaust

In the previous two chapters, we considered the unique role that language plays in human existence. We saw how, for human beings, language is not just a tool used for designating things in the world but fundamentally shapes the kind of world that we live in. The profound changes that happen to our lives as we acquire language are a testament to this point. Language becomes for us a source of understanding, of meaning, and of new ends. We, in turn, become the kind of creature who seeks out these discoveries, what I have referred to as a linguistic being. This transformation is profound. It is also ongoing. We do not just become linguistic beings at some point in childhood; we continue this *becoming* for the rest of our lives. In turn, the language we come to inhabit is not simply a set of unchanging ideas overdetermining our understanding of the world. For no act of speech, however eloquent or precise, ever has the final word.

When philosophers in the tradition of hermeneutic phenomenology, then, insist on the need for interpretation as a basic feature of texts, it is this understanding of language that they have in mind. For hermeneutic phenomenology, understanding a text often requires the bidirectional movement described in the previous chapter. It requires that we project beyond what is immediately given in the text and that we then put the meanings that emerge from this projection to the test. In this way, the activity of reading mirrors what occurs in genuine conversation. Indeed, such projection is, for this tradition, a regular feature of our everyday lives. When engaged in genuine conversation with friends, we project ourselves ahead of the individual words and sentences they utter in order to think along with them. We project some understanding of what it is they are talking about and what, in general, they want to say. Likewise, when we read a book, we do not just read to receive information from the author, but to think along with the author about the topic at hand. In these ways, language regularly solicits from us what Gadamer calls understanding [*Verstehen*].

We know, of course, that not every instance of language that we encounter solicits us in this way. Much of it is immediately intelligible to us. But are there certain kinds of writing that tend to engage us in the hermeneutic process of understanding? Beyond this, are there specific life experiences that compel a person to engage in such writing? Now on this last question, it would seem that phenomenology itself has little to say. The question is, after all, about the worldly occurrences that might compel or cause a certain kind of writing to occur. For Husserl, though, phenomenological inquiry must bracket consideration of causal questions,[1] a point that Heidegger reiterates when he insists on a strong distinction between ontological and ontic inquiry and relegates all anthropological, psychological, and biological investigations into human behavior to the latter category.[2]

The question naturally arose, however, to twentieth-century Continental philosophers as they began to grapple with the literature of the Holocaust. In the aftermath of the Holocaust, many survivors turned to writing to bear witness to what had transpired when friends and family members suddenly went missing in the night or when they themselves labored and starved in the Nazi camps. Continental philosophers, coming out of the phenomenological tradition, read these works and recognized that these texts in particular placed a demand on all those who read them. The texts left behind were, after all, often cryptic and self-effacing. Their authors struggled to find adequate language for what they experienced, as they struggled to discover any coherence or meaning in the tragedy. Some mark this failure in their writings, and some speak about it in their own commentary on their work. Moreover, the sense of failure for many writers was heightened by memories of intense linguistic alienation in the camps or as a survivor in postwar Europe. Present in the writings of Robert Antelme, Paul Celan, and Primo Levi, these patterns have drawn the interest of a number of Continental philosophers, including Gadamer, Maurice Blanchot, Judith Butler, Jacques Derrida, Sarah Kofman, Emmanuel Levinas, and Jean-Francois Lyotard, each of whom has written on what compelled this writing and on the social and philosophical response that it demands.

In this chapter, then, I want to explore how some of these interpretations of Holocaust literature helped to shape Continental philosophy of language. Although the historical moment that is marked by this body of literature is undoubtedly singular, the philosophical response to the literature of the Holocaust also helped to shape Continental philosophy of language for decades to come. As I will argue here, it encouraged Continental philosophers like Blanchot and Derrida to consider why survivors of traumatic experiences so often turn to writing as a way of recovering meaning in the wake of trauma, and what role others have, as readers and listeners, in this process of recovery. Moreover, in examining the suffering that can occur when, through trauma, one becomes alienated from language, we will begin in this chapter to explore the vulnerability of our linguistic being and how attention to such vulnerability helps bring to light the essential role of language in human flourishing.

THE WRITING OF TRAUMA AS A WAY OF UNDERSTANDING

Nobody over the past century did more than Maurice Blanchot to bring a serious and sustained reflection on literary writing to philosophy. Besides novels, Blanchot produced several major works on the subject of writing. Notable among these are *The Work of Fire* (1943), *The Space of Literature* (1955), *The Infinite Conversation* (1969), and *The Writing of the Disaster* (1980). Some of these volumes contain the kind of argumentative essays that are the standard for the genre of philosophy. Their adherence to a standard philosophical style of argument, for example, makes *The Space of Literature* and *The Infinite Conversation* his most accessible works for a philosophical audience. Others, like *The Writing of the Disaster*, are comprised of fragments and thus are less accessible to traditional philosophical readers. All of these works, however, are reflections on the modern literary experience and, in particular, on the experience of those writers in the modern era, like post-Holocaust authors, for whom language serves a redemptive function.

In *The Space of Literature*, for example, Blanchot examines Franz Kafka's experience of the need to write as recounted in his diaries. Like other modern writers that Blanchot discusses (such as Mallarmé, Valéry, and Rimbaud), Kafka had a tremendous sense of urgency about writing and spoke of it often as a means essential to his survival and sense of place in the world. In a 1914 entry that Blanchot discusses, for example, Kafka makes note of the life-changing events quickly transpiring around him as the war intensifies. In his journal entry, Kafka notes that, with the development of the war, he is more determined than ever to write; as he puts it, "I will write despite everything, at any price: it is my fight for survival."[3] Kafka's words here capture well what has interested Blanchot throughout his life—the experience of an urgent *demand to write* and the question of what gives rise to this demand. It is from the standpoint of this question that Blanchot examines the phenomenon of modern literature and, with it, the literature of the Holocaust.

Why then, generally speaking, do we write? I mean writing here as an intransitive verb—the kind of writing that fascinates Walker Percy, which, as we saw in the first chapter, leads him to marvel at what a peculiar creature the human being is. I mean the kind of writing that appears to us, as we write, to be its own end. Why do we do this kind of writing? It is common for us today to think about this demand as the need to express something personal, that is, to bring something that is privately weighing on a person out into the open, to be shared with others. Indeed, this is usually how we understand the point of writing a journal. However, Blanchot suggests that for the modern writer, the impetus of writing is something quite different, even opposite, from this. The modern writer writes, Blanchot says, so that the world might recede and fall silent.[4] The writer does not embark on a journey inward, does not write to know himself better or to express personal experiences. The point is not about representing the immediate "I" or its experiences, but about transforming experience through a kind of negation. In *The Space of Literature*, Blanchot describes this as the essential function of language. Drawing from Mallarmé's distinction between two kinds of language, Blanchot explains: "Crude speech 'has a bearing upon the reality of things.' 'Narration, instruction, even description' give us the presence of things, 'represent' them. The essential word moves them away, makes them disappear. It is always allusive; it suggests, evokes."[5]

To most, this will sound like a very peculiar interpretation of writing. After all, we don't usually think about writing as an act of negation—one that leaves us with less wonder, less meaning, less understanding, and so on. Blanchot, however, does not conceive of the writer's activity as a purely negative procedure in this sense. Instead, he sees writing as enacting a more *determinate* negation in the Hegelian sense. For Hegel, thinking and, indeed, reality itself proceeds as a series of negations, for instance, the negation of untrue forms of consciousness in *Phenomenology of Spirit*. Each of these negations results not in skepticism or pure nothingness but in some new content, in which what is negated is preserved.[6] In this sense, the negations are determinate—producing some positive meaning—rather than simply indeterminate. For Blanchot, Hegel's concept of negation helps to explain that peculiar human experience of wanting to translate life into the written word. In putting itself to the task of writing, human consciousness replaces its former object (the "I" and its immediate experiences) with something new. With this development comes not just a new object for, but also a new *mode of* human consciousness.[7] This new mode of consciousness is the "work."

It is significant that Blanchot talks about "works" and not "texts." The latter became the preferred term for Continental theorists in the poststructuralist tradition such as Derrida and Roland Barthes. Barthes makes much, in fact, of why we ought to prefer the term "text" to "work" in his essay, "From Work to Text."[8] However, Blanchot uses "work" because he is interested precisely in the independent being of the object that the labor of writing produces. A writer producing a work does not simply convey the experiences of a subject, but transforms these things into something new, and in so doing transforms the writer's relationship to these things as well.

But, for Blanchot, where does the need for such a transformation come from? In *The Infinite Conversation*, Blanchot describes how language in general serves the purpose of capturing what is more stable and permanent among that stream of fleeting impressions that make up our first-order experience. This is true for writing but also, at a more basic level, for linguistic concepts themselves. Linguistic concepts—like "work," and "immediacy"—give us ways to gather experience together to form new objects of knowledge that have relative stability over time. It is thus the fleetingness of experience that requires this general transformation. In *The Infinite Conversation* and *The Space of Literature*, Blanchot describes this fleetingness of experience metaphorically as a kind of "death" that is built into human experience and to which we are naturally compelled to respond. The response provided by language is not, however, a simple refusal of this "death" but the transformation of it. This is clear, for example, in the case of concept development. Blanchot explains:

> The force of the concept does not reside in refusing the negation that is proper to death, but on the contrary in having introduced it into thought so that, through negation, every fixed form of thought should disappear and always become other than itself. Language is of a divine nature, not because it renders eternal by naming, but because, says Hegel, "it immediately overturns what it names in order to transform it into something else" . . . in order to reduce it to the unyielding work of the negative through which, in an unceasing combat, meaning comes toward us, and we toward it.[9]

For Blanchot, then, the demand to write issues from human experience itself. It is an attempt to capture what risks being lost in the constant flow of first-order experience. Thus, one need not have experienced the loss of a particular person, place, or life goal to be claimed by the urge to write. This, after all, was not the primary motivation to write for people like Kafka, Mallarmé, or Rimbaud. The demand to write can issue from any kind of life at all, for writing is precisely the attempt to work through human experience in all of its accidental character.

That said, given Blanchot's point about the fleetingness of experience, it would only make sense that the demand to write would be especially pronounced whenever one senses that a valuable experience, idea, or element of the imagination is at risk of disappearing. When we go through something difficult, confusing, or unsettling, many of us try to make sense of what we have experienced through writing. By expressing it in language, we hope to bring the experience into new focus, seeing it in terms of what we feel we know better, leaving us less unsettled. We tend to write more when we are traveling, for example. This is not only to preserve valuable experiences that we have while away, but because traveling tends to instill in us a sense for the fleetingness of things, this stirs us to write. Many people also feel compelled to write as a way of coming to terms with the death of a loved one. In this case, we are not attempting to substitute a set of remarks, say, in a eulogy, for the person we have lost, but we are attempting to find them in a new form and through a transformed mode of relation. Blanchot's work thus sheds light on why we are compelled to work through such losses with words, and what we mean to accomplish through such work. In writing, we find determinacy and meaning where previously there was none. In this way, writing is pivotal to how human beings reorient themselves after they have lost their footing in the world.

To Blanchot, this became especially apparent as he grappled with the writing that emerged out of the experiences of the Holocaust. This was, after all, a time of profound loss—loss of those who were starved, gassed, shot, or worked to death by the SS, and loss of hope in the masses of humanity that allowed it to happen. It was a time of great anxiety about what future generations would remember and learn from the Holocaust. It was also a time in which many survivors like Blanchot, who only narrowly escaped execution by the Nazis in 1944, struggled with the guilt of having survived what so many others did not—a guilt accompanied by a profound sense of justice's absence from the world. [10] This guilt even affected many of those who survived the camps. Primo Levi, for example, struggled after liberation with the torment of having survived, plagued by a sense that he had usurped the place of others. [11] It is not surprising, then, that many survivors, like Levi himself, eventually took their own lives.

The Holocaust thus robbed those who survived it of the world that they knew. The people, the social institutions, and the ways of under-standing that had anchored them in their lives had either disappeared or had come to appear to them as precarious and fleeting. Many who sur-vived these atrocities, then, felt a need to put the terrible ordeal into language. Through documentation, the experiences would be preserved for future reflection. They would be preserved—not so that the wounds of these profound losses would stay open, subjecting future generations to the same violence survivors themselves endured. Instead, through speaking and writing about them, survivors could distill from these trau-matic experiences a new object of consciousness, finding some determi-nate meaning in them that could be passed on to others.

But here too, Blanchot insists, the demand to write was not a matter of simply conveying these traumatic experiences as they were experienced. Regarding Robert Antelme's *The Human Condition*, for instance, Blanchot explains: "It is not . . . simply a witness's testimony to the reality of the camps or a historical reporting, nor is it an autobiographical narrative. It is clear that for Robert Antelme, and very surely for many others, it is a question not of telling one's story, of testifying, but essentially of *speaking*."[12]

What distinction is Blanchot drawing here? For Blanchot, Antelme's need to speak of Dachau did not amount to a need to replay his memories of Dachau. Returning to the scene of trauma, after all, would be unbearable for a survivor. Trauma undoes the sense of self and wreaks havoc on one's ability to make sense of the world. It makes the world feel intensely unpredictable and undoes one's confidence in finding meaning in it. Writers like Antelme, then, wanted to speak not as a way of simply representing their memories to others, but as a way of converting traumatic memories into something new and thus relating to them in a new way. Their writing was like the speech of eulogy in this way. It provided a way to testify to loss while preserving what has been lost in a new way. It was in this way that such writing served a therapeutic function for these authors. For as Butler explains of Levi's writing, it was the substitution of a story for his raw memory, what she terms the "crystallization" of traumatic memory, that was necessary for Levi in the aftermath of his experiences at Auschwitz.[13] It is this writing, then, that is non-immediate in the sense described in the previous chapter, as it provides neither the reader nor even the author with unmediated access to the original experience that prompted the writing. Indeed, for Blanchot, it is the movement of negation, the negation of that original experience, that constitutes the work of these texts and provides a primary motivation for these authors to write.

THE LINGUISTIC ALIENATION OF TRAUMA: THE CASE OF PAUL CELAN

Perhaps no other writer who emerged from the tragedy of the Shoah better expressed the experience of the demand to write than Paul Celan. Celan's poems are undoubtedly expressions of profound loss. They are attempts to give expression to the traumatic events that Celan, born Paul Antschel, experienced during the Third Reich. Celan's parents were deported from their home in 1942 to an internment camp in Transnistria, where his father died of typhus and his mother, as Celan later learned, was shot in the neck. Many of Celan's poems grieve the loss of his parents. Others address the loss of close friends. Another, the loss of his firstborn son. And beyond these personal losses, there is good reason to read many of Celan's poems as mourning all victims of the Holocaust as well as the disappearance of a grounding trust in humanity that Celan lost through the atrocities of the Third Reich and never regained.

But, like Antelme's writing, Celan's poems do not just describe these traumatic losses. Instead, writing was a way to work through them. Celan makes this point in his Bremen Address ("Speech on the Occasion of Receiving the Literature Prize of the Free Hanseatic City of Bremen") when he speaks about the way language anchored and oriented him through the incredible losses he suffered. Writing poems, he explains, was a way to "orient myself, to find out where I was and where I meant to go, to sketch out reality for myself [*um mir Wirklichkeit zu entwerfen*]."¹⁴ What Celan describes here is the essential, world-formative capacity of human language that, as we saw in the first chapter, Heidegger and Percy found so important. Recall that, when examined phenomenologically, language is not just a tool for referring and communicating, but is basic to the constitution of the world in which we dwell. It is largely through language that we orient ourselves in a world and sketch out a reality for ourselves, and this is why language is, as we have seen, of such central importance to the kind of existence that we have as human beings.

But does such a model of language really capture what is taking place in the literature that emerges from survivors of the Holocaust? One might object here that it is this normal capacity that we have as linguistic beings that is severed when one undergoes trauma. Trauma indeed wreaks havoc on the trust we typically put into language to make sense of things and to settle the meaning of our experiences.¹⁵ With trauma, one undergoes an experience of violence that is either so sudden (e.g., deportation, rape, physical assault, the sudden forced separation from one's family) or so totally dehumanizing (e.g., enslavement, incarceration, or internment in a death camp) that one is unable to make sense of or psychologically defend oneself against the loss.

The objection is an important one, since it is, indeed, common for a victim of trauma to lose the sense of self as a linguistic being. If, for example, in being assaulted, I feel myself suddenly reduced to a mere object for another, deprived of any ability to address or be recognized as a subject by my assailant, then I will suffer a profound alienation from myself as a linguistic being. Likewise, if through state-organized incarceration and detainment, I lose my ability to form or retain social relations, come and go freely, exercise moral conscience, and protest against, flee from, or otherwise fend off assaults and violations to my person, then I will suffer not just these harms themselves but the additional loss of linguistic being.

Robert Antelme explains that such deprivation was one part of what made the camps so dehumanizing. He describes, for example, the profound alienation he experienced when addressed by the SS during the roll call each day at Dachau:

A Lagerschutz calls out the names, butchering them. In among them, amid Polish and Russian names, is my name. Laughter when my name is called, and I reply "Present." It sounded outlandish in my ear, but I'd recognized it. And so for one brief instant I'd been directly designated here, I and no other had been addressed, I had been specially solicited—I, myself, irreplaceable! And there I was. Someone turned up to say yes to this sound, which was at least as much my name as I was myself, in this place. And you had to say yes in order to return into the night, into the stone that bore the nameless face. Had I said nothing, they would have hunted for me, and the others would not have left until I had been found. They would have had a recount, they would have seen that there was one who hadn't said yes, one who didn't want that to be him. Then, having found me, the SS would have worked me over so as to make it clear to me that here being me really meant being me, and so as I'd have the logic good and straight in my head: that, around here, I was damned well I, and this nothing that bore the name that had been read out was damned well me.[16]

Here we see one of the ways that linguistic alienation was a part of the trauma that Antelme experienced. To answer to his name, to participate in this linguistic exchange administered by the SS, would be to confirm the reality of what was transpiring; thus, the prisoner's reluctant participation in the forced exchange. Traces of this linguistic alienation are present in Antelme's writing. Kofman notes, for example, the frequency of the impersonal pronoun "one" in Antelme's text, which she argues underscores how the prisoner loses his ability to say "I" as well as the space of interpersonal address in which he would use "I" in conversation with another. Kofman observes that the pronoun "I" appears only rarely in Antelme's writing, and when it does, usually shows up as "a defensive reaction against 'coagulation' and anonymity, when Antelme is describing the loss of identity of the detainee."[17] Here his words were reduced to an instrument with which the SS exerted control over his life. His organs of speech, usually the locus of transcendence, became a means through which he was cruelly reduced to mere facticity, to the object of an irrational power. One thinks here of Elaine Scarry's description of torture, where torturers "mime the work of pain by temporarily breaking off the voice, making it their own, making it speak their words, making it cry when they want it to cry, be silent when they want its silence, turning it off and on, using its sound to abuse the one whose voice it is as well as other prisoners."[18] This particular form of agony, one that Antelme knew well, is captured in the title of Kofman's book: *Smothered Words* [*Paroles suffoquées*].

Wreaking havoc upon our sense of ourselves as linguistic beings, traumatic experience appears to be precisely the kind of thing that "smothers" language, that speech cannot easily settle for us. Traumatic experiences leave us, instead, speechless. Moreover, as Susan Brison explains, the effects of trauma remain long after the physical threat is gone.[19] Just as the survivor tends to suffer from a heightened sense of physical vulnerability in the aftermath of the traumatic experience, so too do many survivors experience a diminished sense of linguistic being as a long-term symptom of trauma.

Why, then, did so many survivors—Antelme, Celan, Levi—turn to writing after the Holocaust? And what could it mean when Celan describes, not just writing, but language in general as the one stable, reliable thing that he could turn to throughout the trauma and its aftermath? "Reachable, near and not lost," Celan says, "there remained in the midst of the losses this one thing: language."[20] How is it, then, that language remained a means of orienting himself as Celan tried to navigate a life haunted by a persistent sense of irresolvable loss?

Blanchot's analysis of the demand to write can help us up to a point. Recall that, for Blanchot, the demand to write is bound up with the movement of negation and is to some extent an attempt to work through loss. What this involves is not denying loss and replacing it with some substitute representation, but a determinate negation of immediate experience. This helps explain why post-Holocaust writers like Celan, Levi, and Kofman refrained from writing in a purely documentary style, one that presented itself as an unadulterated memory of past events. It sheds light on Celan's remarks in his Bremen Address as well, where he tells his audience that "language, remained, not lost, yes in spite of everything. But it had to pass through its own answerlessness, pass through frightful muting, pass through the thousand darknesses of deathbringing speech [*todbringender Rede*] . . . 'enriched' by all this."[21] It is this aspect of Celan's poetics that captured the interest of Blanchot, like so many other Continental philosophers of language.

On the other hand, the work of negation seems never to come to completion for Celan. He seems never to have managed to work through his loss completely, and his poor mental health, his hospitalizations, and eventually his suicide in Paris in 1970 all attest to the fact that, for Celan, the demand to write was never satisfied. One is tempted here to use an image from one of Celan's poems and say that the wounds he suffered did not "scar over [*vernarben*]" but remained open.[22] This conclusion is suggested too by the repetition of negative formulations in "Psalm," "The Sluice," "An Eye, Open," and the untitled poem beginning "Aspen Tree"—a repetition that supplies each of these poems with its distinctive rhythm. In these instances, the negation does not seem determinate. It does not seem to resolve itself into new meaning.[23] The transformation of the loss into a work seems to remain *underway*. They speak, yes, but seemingly only of the absence of a proper account of what has been lost and of the strain on language as it tries to give this account. We find, for example, in the following lines a palpable ambiguity in the poet's relationship to language.

Nowhere are you asked after—The place where they lay, it has a name—it has none.[24]

[*Nirgends fragt es nach dir—Der Ort, wo sie lagen, er hat einen Namen—er hat keinen.*]

You my words go with me going crippled, you my straight ones.[25]

[*Ihr meine mit mir verkrüppelnden Worte, ihr meine geraden.*]

These words attest to a kind of linguistic alienation, that is, a significant disruption in one's capacity as a linguistic being. To be sure, the linguistic alienation presented here differs in significant ways from Antelme's experience in Dachau, but still appears here in a way that seems to make the *work* of these poems appear incomplete. In the first line, from the poem "Stretto," Celan both confirms and denies the naming of a loss. To name the place where the dead lie would be to consecrate the loss and to hold it in memory. For Celan, though, the place is both consecrated and not consecrated, remembered and forgotten.

From this discussion, we might conclude that a trauma like the one that Celan endured brings language to its limit. We might even argue that such a case calls into question the general claim that I developed in the previous chapter, namely, that language plays an essential role in what allows a human being to flourish. What, then, does Celan mean when he says that language remained despite everything?

To get a more complete answer to this question, we need to go further into a dimension of linguistic being that we have only touched on up to this point, that is, the interpersonal. What we will see is that, for Celan, the demand to write issued from a distinctly interpersonal need that linguistic beings possess. This is the need to *bear witness* to loss, to find an empathetic other that will listen and, as part of this listening, engage in the process of interpretive understanding described in the previous chapter. This, I will argue, is why Celan's poems so often feel like works still underway toward their destination. It is not just that Celan found it difficult to speak about his experiences. Like many trauma survivors who begin to speak and write about their experiences, he used his poetry as a way of addressing others who might listen, and he did this as a way of working through trauma.

DERRIDA ON THE POEM AS INTERPERSONAL ADDRESS

Losing trust in others is a common symptom experienced by trauma survivors. In Celan's case, it was crippling—so intense that it ruined many of his closest relationships and contributed to the instability that eventually led to his suicide. The struggle also appears very evidently in his poems, which speak often of the absence of witnesses to suffering and the absence of memorialization for the victims of the Holocaust. In speaking of absence, these poems seem to perform not a determinate negation as described above, but rather an indeterminate one. Rather than articulating a new form of consciousness that emerges as one grapples with such loss, the poems seem to cut off any such development—marking what has not and perhaps cannot be understood about what happened. In his book on Celan's poetry, *Sovereignties in Question*, Derrida suggests that Celan's poems "seal" themselves up in various ways, withholding something from the reader even as they are read. This happens, for example, through the frequent use of a seemingly untranslatable idiom but also, Derrida argues, through the observation that the poems "may refer to events to which the German language will have been a privileged witness, namely, the Shoah."[26]

Despite this, Derrida points out, the poems still function as a powerful act of communication. Steeped as they are in an encrypted idiom and referring, as they seem to do, to a singular set of experiences, they manage nevertheless to bear witness. Indeed, Derrida concludes from his reading of Celan that "all responsible witnessing engages a poetic experience of language."[27] But what does it mean that one cannot bear witness responsibly without engaging in this kind of poetic experience? Consider the following stanza written by Celan, which serves as the basis for Derrida's reflection in his essay. The stanza reads:

> Ash-aureole behind . . .
> No one
> bears witness for the
> witness.[28]
> [*Aschenglorie hinter* . . .
> *Niemand*
> *Zeugt für den Zeugen.*]

On the face of it, these words seem to attest to an absolute alienation—to Celan having lost all hope in bearing witness. After all, here we see the use of an indeterminate form of negation: *Niemand*. Nobody can bear witness for the witness, the survivor of the Holocaust. The survivor will find nobody with whom to share what happened, who will understand. If this is what is meant, then the survivor's experience and testimony would seem to return to the fleeting passage of all things, to that which, according to Blanchot, writing was supposed to offer some meaning and resolution.

Let us look more closely at how the attempt at translation reveals the hermetic quality of the poem, according to Derrida. Looking at the translation of the poem from one idiom to the other, we can see that some words in the poem would present real challenges to translators. *Zeugen*, for example, can mean not only to bear witness but to engender, to procreate, or to father. Neither the English word *witness* nor the French word *témoin* carries this meaning. What's more, Celan's term *Aschenglorie*, as a neologism, has no direct equivalent, and sounds cryptic even in German.

Like the rest of his neologisms, they make up part of Celan's unique idiom.[29] The idiomatic nature of Celan's poems is thus one way that they caution us to respect their singularity.

The other way that the poems do this, as mentioned above, has to do with their reference to singular events. Now, one might want to say that Celan's poems cannot be witnessed by another in that they refer to a first-person experience that nobody else can stake a claim to, not even another survivor whose firsthand experience would be his own. This may strike us as important to acknowledge so as not to overlook important differences between the experiences of, say, Celan and Derrida, or Celan and Blanchot. At the same time, it is also important to keep in mind what we have been establishing about the writing of trauma, namely, that the survivor-writer must not simply retain the traumatic experience in its original form as the object of his writing, but must transform it. As such, in Celan's poems we find more allusion to the events of the Holocaust rather than direct, unequivocal reference. Moreover, by alluding to the events and encrypting the language used to express these events, Celan's poems invite readers to engage in the process of understanding as they read and interpret. Where the language leaves off, they press on. Where the idiom is sealed, they translate. The poems invite readers, in other words, to participate in what I have called the living life of language.

For Derrida, then, these features do not resign the author to an absolute linguistic alienation. Rather, they allow for texts that claim us as readers, that call for the work of understanding. We explored the meaning of understanding in this sense in the previous chapter. There we emphasized that we have understanding of a text, for example, not when we have an accurate mental representation of the words on the page or even the intentions of the author but when we are able to think along with the text, entering into conversation with it. It is, we argued, as conversation that language is fundamental to our hermeneutic situation. Given this, it is not hard to see why the act of translation, and in particular the translation of a text whose terms have no ready-to-hand equivalent in the language into which the text is translated, requires this kind of understanding. To translate, as Gadamer argues, one must think along with the author that one is translating. Thus, it is only by joining the author in a line of thinking that a good translation is produced.[30] The text in need of translation is, then, like the text woven with allusions. Both come to us "sealed." Thus, Derrida argues, both allow for that act of understanding that is the central topic of investigation in Gadamer's hermeneutic phenomenology.[31]

Derrida clarifies this point by comparing what happens in the poem to what happens when one acts as a witness in a court of law. In both cases, the non-immediacy of what is being recounted or described might be seen to threaten the reliability of the speech-act. What Derrida shows instead is that neither speech-act could exist except by virtue of this non-immediacy. The speech-act of testimony, Derrida points out, requires a kind of oath on the part of the witness and a kind of faith on the part of the audience. He clarifies: "Bearing witness appeals to the act of faith, and thus takes place in the space of pledged or sworn word, or of a promise engaging responsibility before the law, a promise always open to betrayal, always hanging on the possibility of perjury, infidelity, or abjuration."[32] Although to this day personal testimony continues to function as evidence in courts of law, testimony differs in this way from other forms of evidence (what Derrida refers to as "proof"). There is an interpersonal dynamic that is vital to its functioning. In bearing witness, I am not just reporting on events according to memory. I must attest before my audience to my own sincerity and, thus, self-presence. And nobody can do this for me. I must bear witness, in other words, to my own consciousness, swear to what I saw, heard, touched, felt, and so on, and it is this act of swearing that establishes my testimony as credible.[33]

Now, it may be surprising, given Derrida's general unwillingness to take for granted the concept of the subject and its concomitant moral demands, that he acknowledges an authority of self-presence here. He even goes so far in this essay as to say that all responsibility hangs on self-presence, that it would not exist without it. The type of self-presence that he has in mind, though, is not only one that is "coextensive with presence to other things, with having been present" but also, he adds, "to the presence of the other."[34] When, for example, I am asked to tell the truth, to promise, or to swear, it is by others that I am called to self-presence — to attest, for example, to my sincerity and good faith. I am not constantly in a state of presence to myself. Moreover, promises, oaths, witness accounts, and so on requires an addressee, another with whom one shares a world. So, while nobody may testify in the place of another — to witness for the witness — self-presence in this case is emphatically also other-presence.

We can see now why, in his reading of Celan, Derrida concludes that "all responsible witnessing engages a poetic experience of language." When I read a poem as wanting to speak, as having something to say, I know that I cannot take the text as immediate, that I must grapple with it to determine what it wants to say. This is why it exerts a personal claim on me. Likewise, when I hear another's testimony, I recognize that, even as I listen to what is being said and allow myself to be persuaded and moved, the experience of which the witness speaks is alien to me. It is an experience that is not mine and will not become mine, even as I listen. In this sense, I can only bear witness for the witness by affirming these limits, knowing that I cannot speak in the other's place.

For Derrida, then, the fact that there is no witness for the witness turns out to be the very condition for the possibility of bearing witness. It is only one whose experience is not my own that I can hear bearing witness. Likewise, it is not the text whose meaning is completely ready-to-hand that we truly read, as it is the non-immediacy of the text that is the very condition for the possibility of truly reading. As Gadamer says, we read a text not simply through our preconceptions but by having our preconceptions challenged, which is to say, by listening.[35]

But this means that the person on the other side of each of these interactions also knows something of this kind of interpersonal exchange as well. They write in anticipation of others. When they bear witness, similarly, they do so only in relation with others. In this sense, their own words are, for them, underway. This is nowhere clearer than in the case of post-Holocaust literature, in which the choice to write indicated a continued connection with others, a continued desire to address and to be understood by others. Such connection was no doubt put to the test by the traumas endured during the Holocaust. And yet it was to this connection that survivors returned again and again in hope and desperation. Kofman explains that this is why, despite the drastic alienation from language that people like Antelme experienced in the camps, it remained necessary for the prisoners to talk with one another. Such exchanges, Kofman writes, "made it possible for each of them to maintain within himself, in spite of everything, the presence of the other [*autrui*], the responsibility within each for the other's will to stay alive; they made it possible to rediscover the meaning of 'we.'"[36]

Through Derrida's reading of Celan's poetry, then, we can better understand the role that linguistic alienation plays in the life of the linguistic being as well as in Continental philosophy of language. Linguistic alienation is an important part of trauma. It results from traumatic experience and, like other long-term effects of trauma, can linger with a survivor long after the violence has subsided. When present, then, it plays a significant role in the human relationship to language. Continental philosophers like Derrida have rightly given their attention to those authors and texts that bear the traces of such alienation. Yet, as Derrida emphasizes in his reading of Celan, it is also clear that what Blanchot calls "the demand to write" persists even through this painful life condition. As Celan says, the poem is *both lonely and underway.* "The poem wants to reach an Other," Celan tells us, "it needs this other, it needs an Over-against. It seeks it out, speaks toward it."[37] Linguistic alienation is, then, the exception that proves the rule. It deepens rather than diminishes the need that one has for acts of empathetic understanding that sustain us as linguistic beings, and allows us to recognize more acutely than ever just how vital to our existence is the capacity for speech.

NOTES

1. Edmund Husserl, *Ideas: General Introduction to Pure Phenomenology*, trans. W. R. Boyce Gibson (New York: Collier-Macmillan, 1962), 100.

2. Martin Heidegger, *Being and Time*, trans. John Macquarrie and Edward Robinson (New York: Harper & Row, 1962), 71–75.

3. Quoted in Maurice Blanchot, *The Space of Literature*, trans. Ann Smock (Lincoln: University of Nebraska Press, 1982), 63.

4. Ibid., 41.

5. Ibid., 39.

6. G. W. F. Hegel, *Phenomenology of Spirit*, trans. A. V. Miller (Oxford: Oxford University Press, 1977), 51–52. For a helpful discussion of determinate negation, see also Miles Hentrup, "Self-Completing Skepticism: On Hegel's Sublation of Pyrrhonism," *Epoché: A Journal for the History of Philosophy* 23, no. 1 (2018): 105–23.

7. On this point, Blanchot follows Hegel's argument in the introduction to *Phenomenology of Spirit*, where Hegel writes: "In the alteration of the knowledge, the object itself alters for it too, for the knowledge that was present was essentially a knowledge of the object: as the knowledge changes, so too does the object, for it essentially belonged to this knowledge." Hegel, *Phenomenology of Spirit*, 54.

8. Roland Barthes, "From Work to Text," in *The Rustle of Language*, trans. Richard Howard (Berkeley: University of California Press, 1989), 56–64.

9. Maurice Blanchot, *The Infinite Conversation*, trans. Susan Hanson (Minneapolis: University of Minnesota Press, 1993), 35.

10. Blanchot conveys this story in his short essay, "The Instant of My Death." In telling the story, Blanchot chooses to write in the third person so as to mark the strangeness of calling this near-death experience his *own* experience. There he speaks about the guilt of having survived with his life when others did not. He writes, "No doubt what began for the young man was the torment of injustice. No more ecstasy; the feeling that he was only living because, even in the eyes of the Russians, he belonged to a noble class. This was war: life for some, for others, the cruelty of assassination." Maurice Blanchot and Jacques Derrida, *The Instant of My Death / Demeure: Fiction and Testimony*, trans. Elizabeth Rottenberg (Palo Alto, CA: Stanford University Press), 7.

11. Primo Levi, *The Drowned and the Saved* (New York: Simon & Schuster, 1986), 69.

12. Blanchot, *The Infinite Conversation*, 134.

13. "The story is there to establish evidence, to acknowledge that there was an enormous, if not unfathomable, loss of life, and to provide the explicit recognition of loss that mourning requires. But if the story makes more remote the memory of suffering and loss, then the story might be said to institute a kind of melancholia in which the suffering and the loss are denied. The story threatens to substitute for the events it relays, and crystallization is the means of that substitution. The substitution comes at the cost of the event, and so it would seem that a certain strict accountability applies: the story is purchased at the expense of the event itself, just as the life of the survivor is understood to come at the expense of the dead." Judith Butler, "Primo Levi for the Present," in *Parting Ways: Jewishness and the Critique of Zionism* (New York: Columbia University Press, 2012), 190.

14. Paul Celan, "Speech on the Occasion of Receiving the Literature Prize of the Free Hanseatic City of Bremen," in *Selected Poems and Prose of Paul Celan*, trans. Joel Felstiner (New York: W. W. Norton, 2001), 396.

15. Elaine Scarry, for example, describes the world-shattering, language-shattering effect of traumatic pain in *The Body in Pain: The Making and Unmaking of the World* (Oxford: Oxford University Press, 1985).

16. Quoted in Sarah Kofman, *Smothered Words*, trans. Madeline Dobie (Evanston, IL: Northwestern University Press, 1998), 45.

17. Ibid., 47.

18. Scarry, *The Body in Pain*, 54.

19. Susan Brison, *Aftermath: Violence and the Remaking of a Self* (Princeton, NJ: Princeton University Press, 2003), 39–40.

20. Celan, "Speech on the Occasion of Receiving the Literature Prize of the Free Hanseatic City of Bremen," 395.

21. Ibid., 395.

22. Paul Celan, "Voices," in *Selected Poems and Prose of Paul Celan*, trans. Joel Felstiner (New York: W. W. Norton, 2001), 93.

23. Magdalena Zolkos offers an interpretation of Celan along these lines, reading his work as an indication of the way that transitional justice narratives can too easily smooth over the impossibility of reconciliation for the traumatized subject. Magdalena Zolkos, "*No Pasarán*: Trauma, Testimony, and Language for Paul Celan," *The European Legacy* 14, no. 3 (2009): 269–82.

24. Paul Celan, "Stretto," in *Selected Poems and Prose of Paul Celan*, trans. Joel Felstiner (New York: W. W. Norton, 2001), 120.

25. Paul Celan, "The Wellspring Rushes," in *Selected Poems and Prose of Paul Celan*, trans. Joel Felstiner (New York: W. W. Norton, 2001), 165.

26. Jacques Derrida, "The Poetics and Politics of Witnessing," in *Sovereignties in Question: The Poetics of Paul Celan*, ed. Thomas Dutoit and Outi Pasanen (New York: Fordham University Press, 2005), 67.

27. Ibid., 66.

28. Derrida presents the poem abridged and elided in this way at the beginning of his essay. The full poem can be found in Derrida's essay and in Felstiner's translation: Paul Celan, "Ash-aureole," in *Selected Poems and Prose of Paul Celan*, trans. Joel Felstiner (New York: W. W. Norton, 2001), 260–61.

29. For an alternative account of the unique idiomatic quality of Celan's poetry, see Alejandro Vallega's *Sense and Finitude*, where he argues that the poet's departure from the normal constraints of grammar and syntax are a way of regenerating language by reactivating its sensuous, prelinguistic roots. Alejandro A. Vallega, *Sense and Finitude: Encounters at the Limits of Language, Art, and the Political* (Albany: State University of New York Press, 2009), 81–101.

30. Derrida follows Gadamer in arguing that translation has its proper place precisely where translation is difficult. This is why, for Derrida, the poem is "the only place propitious to the experience of language, that is to say, of an idiom that forever defies translation and therefore demands a translation that will do the impossible, make the impossible possible in an unheard-of event." Jacques Derrida, "Rams: Uninterrupted Dialogue—Between Two Infinities, the Poem," in *Sovereignties in Question: The Poetics of Paul Celan*, ed. Thomas Dutoit and Outi Pasanen (New York: Fordham University Press, 2005), 137. It should be pointed out, however, that this point of agreement was not properly recognized by Derrida himself.

31. Derrida, "Rams: Uninterrupted Dialogue," 139–40.

32. Derrida, "The Poetics and Politics of Witnessing," 75.

33. This is notoriously difficult to do for survivors of trauma, who are giving testimony to their experience precisely because, as we have seen, there is often a crystallization of memory that takes place in the wake of trauma. Still, Derrida's point is that testimony is not simply about recounting what happened but swearing to be sincere in recounting as best as possible.

34. Derrida, "The Poetics and Politics of Witnessing," 79–80.

35. Hans-Georg Gadamer, *Truth and Method*, trans. Joel Weinsheimer and Donald G. Marshall (London: Bloomsbury, 2004), 282–85.

36. Kofman, *Smothered Words*, 54.

37. Paul Celan, "The Meridian," in *Selected Poems and Prose of Paul Celan*, trans. Joel Felstiner (New York: W. W. Norton, 2001), 409.

FOUR

Rethinking Women's Silence

Contributions from Continental Feminism

In the previous chapter, we explored how language plays a role in helping people to work through traumatic experience. This was demonstrated in the work of post-Holocaust writers such as Celan and Antelme, who turned to writing in the wake of the atrocities of the Holocaust. For these survivors, writing was an attempt to work through trauma, recovering meaning where it had previously been lost. Their writing thus exemplifies language's constant role as the essential mode of disclosure for human beings. Yet the efficacy of language in this role, as we saw, hinges on the anticipation of others who share language with us. This is generally true of all writing. As Derrida argues, it is always for another that I write. It is in response to another's address that I bear witness to what I have experienced. It is by another that I am first called to disclose myself in speech. Hence, if we want to support others as linguistic beings, we must take on the role of the empathetic listener. We must "bear witness for the witness," as Derrida says.

This argument has radical implications for how we understand understanding. It suggests, for one, that whenever I speak about myself or my experience, that account is always structured by the others to whom I am responding. Their expectations mediate the accounts of myself that I give, just as they mediate the way that I understand the world. In this way, my language is never simply my own, a reflection of an individual's isolated attempt to make sense of things.

Continental philosophers coming out of the tradition of hermeneutic phenomenology have generally focused on what such mediation enables in our lives. Having the ear of the other compels me to speak. It pushes me to participate in the activity of interpretation. It compels me to bear

63

witness to what I have undergone and to my own self-presence at this moment. These positive effects take place even when I am alone insofar as I anticipate another who will listen. Gadamer reminds us that even the private conversation that we have with ourselves "is always simultaneously the anticipation of conversation with others and the introduction of others into the conversation with ourselves."[1] My potential reader pushes me to articulate ideas, to identify them as my own, and to find new meanings through this process. Being able to anticipate others who can recognize the meaning of what I have to say, then, is essential to my flourishing as a linguistic being. Indeed, we might say that, beyond the freedom to speak, it is access to empathetic listening that is the more fundamental social good, because the former is meaningless without the latter.

Ideally, we enable one another to speak by both listening to others and having them listen to us. In reality, though, our patterns of social communication often lack this reciprocity. What we find is that, in our personal interactions, some people do more talking and receive more of the listening, while others take on the lion's share of the listening and, over time, do much less of the talking. Hermeneutic phenomenology has not traditionally concerned itself with this problem. Given what we have seen so far, however, this pattern, wherever we find it, should be concerning. It should concern us not because it violates some abstract principle of equality, but because it speaks to how people can become alienated from their linguistic being and deprived of what they need to flourish in this capacity. In this chapter, I will examine the way that some feminist philosophers have taken up this issue, focusing particularly on contributions by Continental feminist philosophers. In so doing, my hope is to show not only how conversations in feminist philosophy pose new and important questions relevant to a hermeneutic philosophy of language, but also how important developments in Continental feminist philosophy carry forward some of the key insights of hermeneutic phenomenology.

THE IDEA OF WOMEN'S LANGUAGE IN CONTINENTAL FEMINISM

One might wonder, though, whether the treatment of language in Continental feminist philosophy is really compatible with the account of language that I have offered so far, an account that has been grounded in the insights of hermeneutic phenomenology. Indeed, one may even take as a defining characteristic of Continental feminism a general skepticism toward language that stems from a commitment to identity politics, in which the language we all rely on to understand the world is seen and discounted as "man's language," a set of concepts rooted in male experience and imposed on women. From such a vantage point, language does not appear to be the means by which the world is continually disclosed and the source for new meanings and ends. It is looked at skeptically, suspiciously, as an analogue to power that is rooted in male identity. I want to begin, then, by first discussing how this approach to language emerges in Continental feminism so as to clarify exactly where I see alternative accounts of language being developed by Continental feminist philosophers.

The emergence of identity politics is rightly described as one of the most significant changes to the political landscape in the West over the past half century. Having witnessed the emergence of the gay liberation movement, the Combahee River Collective, the Quebec sovereignty movement, the Scottish National Party, and the like, recent generations have become accustomed to thinking about such movements as essential to the political process. Radical democratic theorists, for example, may equate democracy itself, as Michaele L. Ferguson does, with "the ongoing contestation of the very subject ('the people') whose existence it presupposes."[2] This process, on such a view, is one in which different groups, understanding their own unique interests to have been neglected on the basis of historic subordination or marginalization, campaign for greater power and recognition. When the aim is recognition, such campaigns require acceptance of the premise that the subordinated group is different in significant ways, in its identity and interests, from that of the broader group from which recognition is sought. As Georgia Warnke points out, this feature of identity politics distinguishes it from earlier movements that were guided by an "integrationist ideal." She explains: "In contrast to earlier struggles for civil and political rights, which demanded equal treatment . . . the politics of identity demands that social and political institutions acknowledge and accommodate differences in race, ethnicity, gender, and sexuality."[3]

This change in our conception of the political process emerged hand in hand with certain developments in sociolinguistics and the philosophy of language. As identity politics took hold of the political imaginary, researchers in both the social sciences and humanities applied the popular paradigm to the study of language and found in their research new evidence supporting the theoretical premises of identity politics. This was nowhere clearer than in the academic branch of the women's movement. In the 1970s and 1980s, academia became a battleground for feminist interventions that aimed to rectify the subordination and marginalization of women within the mechanisms of culture, and academia increasingly became an important site for the development of scholarship that shed light on the nature and importance of that subordination. In this context, language became a focus for feminist inquiry—both in academia and beyond.

Major works like Mary Daly's *Gyn/Ecology: The Metaethics of Radical Feminism* (1978) and Dale Spender's *Man Made Language* (1980) argued that women are engrossed in languages and other symbolic structures that bind them in hidden ways to a patriarchal social structure. They present any language developed under conditions of patriarchy, such as the English language, as "literally man made" and "still primarily under male control."[4] In arguing that language is a symbolic structure used to maintain patriarchal power, these writers adhere to a model of language as a finite construction of reality, not unlike the famous model developed by Edward Sapir and Benjamin Lee Whorf.[5] They adhere, in other words, to a model of linguistic determinism. This is evident early on in *Man Made Language*, when Spender writes:

> Each day, we construct the world we live in according to these man made rules. We select, pattern and interpret the flux of events in the attempt to make life meaningful and few of us suspect how deeply entrenched, and arbitrary, these rules are. We impose them on the world so that what we see conforms to what we have been led to see. And one of the crucial factors in our construction of this reality is language.[6]

Like Sapir and Whorf, Spender emphasizes here the constitutive role that language plays in shaping the way we understand the world at even the most basic level. For Spender, though, this constitutive power must be thought of as an analogue to the political hegemony of men, a connection that seemed well-supported by the significant amount of empirical research in the 1970s and 1980s on women as a "muted group."[7] All of this encouraged an increasingly critical attitude toward language within the women's movement.

Adrienne Rich's *The Dream of a Common Language*, containing poems written from 1974 to 1977, is a telling artifact from this period. In the opening lines from its most famous poem, "Cartographies of Silence," Rich describes the frustration of a conversation that is mediated by "so-called common language" where, despite the presence of a seemingly common medium of communication, the participants experience nothing but alienation and disappointment or, as Rich puts it, "the ice-floe split, the drift apart."[8]

In its suspicion regarding the "so-called common language," the poem's imagery became iconic for its age. It was cited frequently by scholars interested in language as a battleground of identity politics and seen by some to be a poetic expression of Muted Group Theory.[9] Indeed, as Rich's poetry touched on two cartographies of silence, that experienced by women and also by lesbians in particular, it was often read as a general argument about the need for identity politics. According to this argument, it is the illusion of a common language—a common means of recognition—that is most vexing for any subordinated group seeking redress, since this covers over the need to acknowledge and accommodate the group in its particularity.

This argument became central to the thinking of several Continental feminist theorists. Indeed, its prominence in the writings of figures like Luce Irigaray and Hélène Cixous gave rise to a new category of feminist theory, commonly termed by anglophone theorists "French feminism" but more accurately referred to as the intellectual movement of *Écriture féminine* ("women's writing"). The theorists of *Écriture féminine* were distinctive in that they took language in particular as a significant, albeit hidden, source of inequality, one that has long rendered women essentially silent. Cixous, for example, describes the impact of a history of writing in which "woman has never *her* turn to speak"[10] and where writing has been organized around a "typically masculine—economy . . . where the repression of women has been perpetuated, over and over."[11] Because of this history of silencing women, Cixous argues that it is impossible to say in advance what women's writing will contain. It will be something new, insurgent, unpredictable.[12] With its emphasis on keeping open the content of women's writing, this utopian claim distinguishes the work of French feminists like Cixous from other proponents of identity politics. However, Cixous nevertheless assures her readers that when women "break out of the snare of silence,"[13] there will be a decisive political transformation in women's lives. Thus, Cixous urges women to write and informs them that, in so doing, they will uncover an authentic self that had become gradually suppressed by the disciplinary mechanisms of patriarchy and, above all, by shame. They will come finally to speak as women, in the language authentic to women as historical subjects.

Such arguments brought to prominence the theoretical writings of some Continental feminists, namely those writings that, like the theories of *Écriture féminine*, reflected the growing shift of political theory toward identity politics. With that shift, however, another branch of Continental feminist philosophy of language becomes less visible, less representative of Continental feminism as a whole. This is a branch that highlights the situation of diverse standpoints, not in order to call into question the validity of all attempts to arrive at communication and mutual understanding in this situation, but to shed light on the social conditions that enable these achievements. It is a branch that understands the importance of examining language as a site of women's subordination, not as a matter of women being enclosed in a finite structure that imposes fixed determinations onto thought. It recognizes the problem of linguistic alienation but avoids equating this with all forms of silence and refrains from taking as its central political goal the reconstruction of woman's authentic voice. This branch of Continental feminist philosophy is one rooted in the hermeneutic tradition.

In the next section, I introduce the version of this argument presented by Judith Butler, a leading figure in Continental feminist theory whose approach to language, I argue, is in many ways more compatible with the hermeneutic tradition than with identity politics.[14] Sharing the critical interest in language taken by writers like Cixous and Spender, Butler is committed to the critical interrogation of discourses presumed to be "common" but which function in exclusionary ways. Unlike these writers, however, Butler is emphatic in her insistence on the inevitable sociality of the speaking subject. For Butler, the speaking subject emerges in response to being addressed by others. Moreover, Butler argues that there are ethical reasons for keeping ourselves open and responsive to address by others throughout our lives. Such claims set Butler apart from many of her counterparts in Continental feminism but carry forward some of the most important aspects of the hermeneutic tradition's approach to language.

GIVING AN ACCOUNT OF ONESELF: BUTLER'S HERMENEUTIC CIRCLE

Butler has made a career for herself by drawing attention to how certain patterns of discourse shape the world we live in. Her early work (*Gender Trouble*, *Bodies That Matter*, *The Psychic Life of Power*, *Undoing Gender*) is especially focused on dominant discourses of sex, gender, and sexuality. This work examines, for example, the role that medical discourse has played in producing the concepts of homosexuality and heterosexuality that we take for granted today.[15] Likewise, it considers how psychiatric discourse has shaped the way that we think about transgendered lives, seeing these lives as needing diagnosis and the legitimation of medical opinion.[16] Her early work even examines the discourse surrounding gay marriage and the way it has impacted our attitude toward different kinship relations and sexual lifestyles, helping to further entrench a problematic distinction between normality and abnormality of kinship relations within the gay community.[17] Through such investigations, Butler remains attentive to the way that discourses can render certain lives less intelligible and therefore less legitimate than others.

Indeed, for Butler, drawing attention to such discourse is the primary task of all critical theory and, thus, of any critical feminist theory. It is this task that she undertakes when, for example, she famously engages in a critical genealogy of the category of sex.[18] While it is common for people today to think about gender as the cultural interpretation of sex, and sex as a category that exists independent of any cultural practices, Butler challenges this way of distinguishing sex and gender. She argues that male and female appear as natural kinds and thus as unavoidable categories within animal life only because of the system of gender. The system of gender pervades social life. My gender plays a significant role in my dating practices; in the way that my partner, my colleagues, and my family relate to me; in the kinds of work that I am encouraged or discouraged from performing; in how that work is interpreted and valued; in the health care that I receive; in the way that I inhabit and move my body; and so forth. In sum, gender has traditionally been a primary way in which we interpret our lives and others interpret us. It is true that, in certain social settings today, gender no longer plays the primary interpretive role it once did, but given how uncomfortable the majority of people still are when they encounter a person whose gender is unclear to them, it is evident that gender still plays a significant, even primary, role in most social settings. It is in this general context in which the categories of male and female are relevant to people in most social settings that sex is given the significance that it has as a natural category. Scientific studies of, say, the different risks of cardiovascular disease for women and men make sense because these are meaningful categories for most people. Most people use these categories in some way to identify themselves (most by simply identifying as one or the other) and so can use the information from these studies to understand their health risks. At the same time, scientific studies that use sexual difference as a starting point are often doing more than this. They can serve to reinforce or even introduce the significance of gender as a means of interpreting ourselves and others. For example, we learn from many books to interpret the challenges we experience in life in terms of struggles that men or women specifically have. So, we might read one of thousands of self-help titles directed toward women, such as *Women Who Think Too Much: How to Break Free of Overthinking and Reclaim Your Life* or *How to Be Happy (Or At Least Less Sad): A Creative Workbook.*[19] That some such books are written by scientists who draw from scientific research to support their findings should not be surprising. As Helen Longino's work has made clear, science is a value-laden enterprise.[20] It works with categories that are significant in our social world. To subject the discourse of sex to a critical genealogy, then, would be to draw attention to the cultural practices and social systems of meaning that have historically propped up this discourse. In so doing, we should be able to see that there is no guarantee that such discourse will always be as meaningful as it was in the past—that thirty years in the future, for example, it will seem appropriate to host "gender reveal" parties or to tailor life advice to women in particular under the assumption that "overthinking" is a woman's problem.

So far, what I have described of Butler's project should be uncontroversial. Running throughout the entirety of Butler's corpus is the unifying thread of critique, and the object of critique for Butler is discourse in its world-disclosive capacity. Students who read Butler's work pick up quite easily on these aspects of discourse. After all, while they tend to be immersed in the discourses that Butler critiques, they are also accustomed to adopting an attitude of suspicion toward discourse. Students in my experience tend to be compelled by constructionist arguments made by writers like Nietzsche who present language as an arbitrary construction, offering access to only an illusory reality, and they interpret Butler's critique of discourse as akin to Nietzsche's project in this way.[21] Students also tend to believe very deeply in an old Romantic notion, one recently reinvigorated with the rise of identity politics, that individuals only really flourish if they manage to achieve an authentic self that exists completely independent of any social norms. Thus, they interpret Butler's critique of the category of sex to mean that the category is *merely* a social construct and that, buried beneath the edifice of this construct, there are real identities that, when embraced, allow one to live life authentically. Understood this way, Butler's version of feminist critique would be indistinguishable from that of Spender, Daly, Irigaray, and Cixous.

Several theoretical features distinguish Butler's approach to the critical examination of language from the approach of these other theorists, though. I present three such points of distinction here, indicating how each marks a significant point of agreement between Butler's thought and the hermeneutic philosophical tradition.

First, Butler acknowledges that the way we inhabit the world is irreducibly social and historical. We begin to interpret the world only after we have been thrown into an intricate set of linguistic practices that interpret the world for us, so that what we often mark as the "beginning" of understanding is not really the point of its origination. This thought is central to what Gadamer, following Heidegger, understood as the "hermeneutic circle," the strange idea that genuine understanding actually develops through interpretative acts that take place on the basis of content that one is thrown[22] into, that is, on the basis of prejudices that are "biases of our openness to the world."[23] Recall that this is also the point Heidegger returns to in his later lectures on language, where he describes the speaking in which we find ourselves entangled whenever we first go to speak.[24] For Butler, too, we inevitably inhabit the world through discourses that we do not ourselves choose and in response to forms of address similarly unchosen.[25] And though she is acutely aware of the distress that this can cause, like the hermeneutic phenomenologist, Butler insists that this aspect of the human condition cannot simply be cast off. When we interpret the world, we inevitably do so from within a hermeneutic circle. We begin to interpret ourselves, for instance, only after we have been interpellated by others. I give an account of what motivated my action only after I have come, through being socialized into moral and legal discourses, to see myself and speak of myself as a responsible subject. The capacity for demonstrating accountability in this way, Butler argues, is an effect of another's address. Similarly, one is encouraged to identify as a woman if one has been continually addressed as female from a very early age. Such identities are not spontaneous, but issue from a discourse that precedes the individuals that come to identify in this way. As we can see, then, even if Butler is sympathetic to the idea that we must look for what is foreclosed by the "so-called common language," she cannot affirm the next step that people like Cixous make, going from there to encourage people to embrace and speak with some voice independent from others. She is much too attentive to the social interactions that go into the development of both identity and speech.

Second, while Butler recognizes that it is impossible to disentangle one's speaking completely from the influence of others, she also rejects the idea that the discourses we inherit exhaustively determine our understanding, a claim that is sometimes put forward by Cixous and Spender, for example. The latter rely at times on a theory of linguistic determinism to explain the vast scope of patriarchal power. Indeed, for Cixous, it is only because patriarchal language has so determined every aspect of the cultural imaginary, including that of women, that it is so difficult to say what a "woman's writing" would entail. But while Butler acknowledges the way we are thrown into meanings that we do not choose, she also sees how the structures we are thrown into come to change over time. Indeed, her point is that there is a lot less stability to these discourses than we might think. In her early work, Butler makes this point by showing how certain ideas come to seem natural when they are reinforced through reiterated performance. Take the term "heterosexual." For Butler, the term comes to seem like a natural and inevitable description when it is used repeatedly over time, for example, in clinical and research settings. But this means that the stability of this term rests on such repetition. Butler highlights this instability as a way of demonstrating the immanent possibility of change, despite the power of discourse to habituate our thinking in certain ways. Later, Butler develops a fuller account of how critique arises and functions as a source of change.[26] In *Giving an Account of Oneself*, Butler argues that, although my understanding of a thing is always mediated by a set of terms, these terms are not beyond revision. In fact, sometimes what I encounter makes me question the terms by which I would otherwise attempt to understand a thing. In this way, the terms of recognition become "subject to a critical opening."[27] These are two of the ways, then, that Butler attempts to account for how discourse comes to change. While Butler remains vigilant about what the "so-called common language" might foreclose, she cannot commit herself to the notion that language is simply a one-sided projection onto things, unresponsive and unchanging. While she is attentive to the way that certain discourses shape our lives, she, like Gadamer, rejects linguistic determinism.[28]

Third, in addition to emphasizing the way we are immersed in a language that is shared with others, Butler also argues for the ethical importance of remaining open to the other's address. This argument is an extension of Butler's theory of critique and is influenced substantially by the ethics of Emmanuel Levinas. For Levinas, my habitual ways of understanding what I encounter in the world are interrupted by the encounter with the other. The encounter makes the terms of recognition that I have available appear inadequate to me. This is why the object of the encounter is "the other" in the sense that it eludes the operations of discursive judgment that I would typically use to understand it. In this sense, "the Other [*Autrui*] remains infinitely transcendent, infinitely foreign [*étranger*]."[29] My relation to the other is, we might say, a relation of non-relation.

It may seem as though this interruption could only arise with the encroachment of some sensory, nondiscursive stimuli, but Levinas argues that it is actually the interlocutory scene that most forcefully brings about this relation of non-relation. This is because a conversation requires one to refrain from reducing the interlocutor to an object to be known. There may certainly be times where the theme or subject matter of some conversation is a person, but this is something very different than engaging that person in conversation. To converse is, as we have seen, to *listen* to someone, taking that person as a source of world disclosure. Levinas explains, "In discourse the divergence that inevitably opens between the other as my theme and the other as my interlocutor, emancipated from the theme that seemed a moment to hold him, forthwith contests the meaning I ascribe to my interlocutor."[30]

It is significant, from a hermeneutic standpoint, that it is within an interlocutory scene, a situation oriented toward mutual understanding, that the relation to the other is most forcefully set forth. This suggests that my relation to the other emerges in the context of trying to understand the world together. I relate to the other as a co-participant in world disclosure. When I do this, I share a world in common with them. The emphasis here on commonality may seem inappropriate, given the Levinasian regard for the absolute alterity of the other. The point, though, is that, whenever I engage in this activity of co-disclosure with another, I must really listen. I must, in other words, take the other as a source of understanding distinct from myself. This is how conversation can aim at the development of mutual understanding while also enabling me to encounter the other as other.

Butler draws from this account in Levinas alongside resources in psychoanalysis (in particular, Jean LaPlanche) to explain how the scene of address puts the speaking subject always in relationship to the other. Butler argues that it is only first by being addressed that we come into language. This is how children first come to speak. I give an account of myself when I am prompted to do so. Yet the enabling condition of address is almost always obscured by the narrative that I give of myself. I rarely acknowledge in the account that I give the way that my account has been shaped by those who have addressed me. In this sense, I remain opaque to myself. As Butler writes, "One enters into a communicative environment as an infant and child who is addressed and who learns certain ways of addressing in return. The default patterns of this relationality emerge as the opacity within any account of oneself."[31]

It is not only in childhood, however, that address plays a formative role in our speech. Address functions this way throughout our lives, interrupting our narratives and continually remapping our sources of world disclosure. Put another way, each scene of address prompts a critical opening that puts a given discourse into question. This applies nowhere more clearly than in the case of discourse that I rely on to understand my interlocutor. In the scene of address, I encounter another whom it seems I cannot (I must not) understand within the existing terms of recognition available to me. After all, if I only encounter others in such terms, I cannot also perceive them as the source of address. What addresses me, insofar as it addresses me, is not an object like other objects. What it demands from me is a critical interrogation of my language, my understanding, up to this point.

It is not hard to see why Butler, like Levinas, argues that being addressed by the other in this way is the necessary condition of any ethical deliberation about how I ought to treat others. Before I can engage in ethical deliberation, I must already have found myself in the world with others, in a state of what Butler calls "unchosen proximity."[32] I must already have received the other's address. Butler argues that we must keep this in mind as we engage in ethical deliberation, since any attempt to negate this condition of unchosen proximity will undermine the ground of ethics itself. For many, though, ethical deliberation proceeds precisely by deciding who I am ethically obligated to among those with whom I share the world. Those who fall outside this sphere then cease to make any claim on me. Indeed, they become virtually unintelligible as subjects with moral status. Even here it is possible that I find myself addressed in unexpected ways, that I encounter the other who falls outside the sphere that I imagine encompasses my moral obligations. It is also possible, though, that I cultivate an attitude of responsivity and openness such that I attune myself to the other's claim. These are then different ways that I can respond to the unchosen proximity of the other.

For Butler, then, to dwell in language means to be thrown into forms of world disclosure that we have not chosen. There is no overcoming such a condition. This means that the goal of linguistic authenticity put forward in the work of authors like Spender and Cixous is untenable. At the same time, Butler also makes clear that dwelling in language means at times finding ourselves responsible for (or, better, responsive to) the discourses into which we find ourselves thrown. This bespeaks a commitment to ongoing critique, one propelled by an interpretive attitude that is responsive to the other's address. This twofold characterization of our relationship to language is essential to Butler's philosophy, just as it is essential to the hermeneutic tradition that Butler draws on. Butler insists that we overlook neither side of this tension—neither the fact that we are immersed in discourse from the start, nor the demand on us to critically examine this discourse. Gadamer, too, was quite clear that we never escape the hermeneutic circle. It is where we start from and where we return to again and again in our attempt to understand. As David Loy puts it, "The life we are thrown into is a storied one where the task of interpretation is unavoidable and always incomplete."[33]

Earlier in the chapter, I said that I wanted to broaden our understanding of the contributions of Continental feminism to the philosophy of language. One might wonder at this point, then, what our hermeneutic condition has to do with feminist philosophy and with women in particular. After all, gender was not a meaningful subject within the seminal works of philosophical hermeneutics. Moreover, as I have tried to explain here, the assumption of linguistic authenticity that so often underwrites identity politics is incompatible in important ways with a hermeneutic understanding of language. But the hermeneutic account fits feminist philosophy well if we think about the importance for feminist philosophy of (1) recognizing and not pathologizing the deep relational bonds that we have with others, and (2) recognizing, at the same time, the need to critically examine these bonds. A hermeneutic approach to discourse thus makes sense for a feminist theorist like Butler, who wants to recognize and even value our social bonds with others while still insisting on the importance of social critique.[34] For some time now, feminist philosophy has pursued these two ends—ends often taken to be incompatible. A hermeneutic philosophy of language, like the one articulated by Butler, can thus be helpful in shedding light on the compatibility of these two commitments and thus the cohesion of the field of feminist inquiry.

It is clear, then, that the hermeneutic theory of language does not apply only to women. It is explicitly a theory about understanding *in general*. Stepping aside from the terrain mapped out by classical philosophical hermeneutics, though, we might consider the different roles that men and women tend to play in the interlocutory exchanges that bring about understanding. Is it the case that women and men on average contribute an equal amount of listening? Do men and women display the same responsiveness to the address of the other, bring the same interpretive attitude to the conversations they enter into? If not, what are the consequences for women?[35] Over the past few decades, researchers in feminist sociolinguistics have produced a number of studies that show a discrepancy in the way that such conversational roles are distributed. In the next section I turn to examine this discrepancy, focusing particular attention on the treatment of the subject by Sandra Bartky, a feminist philosopher who brought together hermeneutic phenomenology and Marxist theory in order to better understand the subordination of women. In turning to Bartky, then, I hope to illustrate another place in Continental feminism where the investigation of language as a site of women's subordination is consistent with the hermeneutic account of language that I have been developing throughout the book.

THE SEXUAL DIVISION OF EMOTIONAL LABOR: BARTKY ON WOMEN AS EMPATHETIC LISTENERS

Bartky's landmark volume, *Femininity and Domination: Studies in the Phenomenology of Oppression*, sheds light on the everyday sources of women's subordination, that is, on the everyday habits that over time contribute to the disempowerment of women. In one of the book's essays, "Feeding Egos and Tending Wounds: Deference and Disaffection in Women's Emotional Labor," Bartky explores how taking on a heavy burden of what she calls "emotional caretaking" leads women to become alienated from the capacities they have as linguistic beings.

What does it mean to provide emotional labor? Bartky explains:

> To give such support, then, is to tend to a person's state of mind in such a way as to make his sinking less likely; it is to offer him comfort, typically by the bandaging up of his emotional wounds or to offer him sustenance, typically by the feeding of his self-esteem. The aim of this supporting and sustaining is to produce or to maintain in the one supported and sustained a conviction of the value and importance of his own chosen projects, hence of the value and importance of his own person.[36]

Women typically do more of this emotional caregiving than men. Indeed, Bartky suggests that it is a willingness to bear the burden of such emotional support that we tend to identify with the virtue of "female tenderness." Arguing, however, that women must locate their subordination "in the duties we are happy to perform and in what we thought were the innocent pleasures of everyday life,"[37] Bartky takes a closer look at the form of disempowerment that so often results when women invest themselves fully in the role of emotional caretaker.

Bartky begins her analysis by considering the answer to this question offered by Marxist feminist writer Ann Ferguson, who argues that men's reliance on women's emotional labor is a form of exploitation that parallels the capitalist's exploitation of workers. Ferguson points out that the expectation for women to act as caretakers is essential to the sexual division of labor and to how women's labor becomes systematically exploited by men.[38] To understand Ferguson's argument, we should be clear about how she is using the term "exploitation." "Exploitation" here refers specifically to a relationship between two parties where one party disproportionately extracts the value produced from another's labor. Ferguson takes the term from Marx's labor theory of value.[39] It is important to clarify that to speak about exploitation in this sense is not to imply that the exploited party feels wronged or harmed by the arrangement, nor that the exploiting party acts with the intention to harm. Both may be the case in a given situation of exploitation, but in the modern world, exploitation usually occurs in relationships that both parties understand for the most part as a free and equal exchange.[40] Theorists often use the concept of exploitation, then, to make clear how a given relationship, despite the appearance of an equal exchange, transfers value disproportionately to one party. The worker believes the wages earned are fair compensation for the work provided, but in fact the capitalist only profits if the value of the work is greater than what the worker is paid. Similarly, Ferguson argues, women often accept a disproportionate burden of caretaking responsibilities in their social relationships with men. They believe their own need for care will still be satisfied by their male partners, even if they provide more, and in many cases women believe that they are fairly compensated in other ways, namely, by being financially provided for and/or being given certain honors and other social entitlements as a valued caretaker. In reality, though, Ferguson argues, relationships built on such a division of labor are problematic in that the one in the role of the primary caretaker ends up giving a lot more than she receives. Men profit in many ways—psychologically, financially, even politically—from the emotional caretaking provided to them by women, and they do little as a whole to reciprocate such care. Women's emotional labor is thus commonly exploited. Again, though, this doesn't mean that men intentionally take advantage of women's care, nor are women who are being exploited in this way conscious of the fact that they are getting a raw deal. As Bartky explains, quoting Ferguson:

> Girls learn "to find satisfaction in the satisfaction of others, and to place their needs second in the case of a conflict." Men, on the other hand, "learn such skills are women's work, learn to demand nurturance from women yet don't know how to nurture themselves." Women, like workers, are caught within a particular division of labor which requires that they produce more of a good—here, nurturance—than they receive in return.[41]

Bartky explains that this kind of caretaking can take many forms. It can involve, for example, a woman putting aside her own interests (or the possibility of developing new interests of her own) and putting aside her own time to support and sustain the interests of her male partner. For example, she may become interested in his hobbies, accompanying him on fishing trips or to football games, activities that he was interested in before they met. She may enjoy doing these things insofar as he enjoys them and she enjoys supporting him. Another form that this pattern might take is a woman deferring to her husband's choices, values, and/or ways of understanding the world. Indeed, this may result from the gradual appropriation of his interests and activities. A wife, for example, may defer to her husband's political standpoint or to his judgment on important decisions (e.g., which house to buy, how to spend the family's summer vacation, whether or not a particular man is an acceptable match for their daughter). There is, of course, a spectrum here, and not all heterosexual couples participating in a sexual division of labor divide up such responsibilities in the same way. But seeing these behaviors on a spectrum allows us to see the common thread among them. In the most extreme case, we have a figure like Teresa Stangl, wife of Fritz Stangl, Kommandant of Treblinka, a Catholic who had moral objections to Nazism and was appalled by her husband's work but "maintained home and hearth as a safe harbor to which he returned when he could."[42] Reflecting on the moral shortcomings of Stangl, Bartky insists, "Few of us would take female tenderness to these lengths, but many of us, I suspect, have been morally silenced or morally compromised in small ways because we thought it more important to provide emotional support than to keep faith with our own principles."[43] Many women have indeed internalized the idea that "standing by your man" regardless of what he does is a virtue for women. Now, it may seem strange to call such behaviors acts of "labor," since acts of deference hardly seem like work. However, the accomplishment of such deference requires the performance of concrete actions, actions that take their toll over time on the one who performs them and that benefit the one for whom they are performed. This becomes even more clear when we consider how the expectation of female caretaking takes a commercialized form in the care and attention expected from nurses, flight attendants, secretaries, and service workers — jobs that are traditionally and still primarily occupied by women.

Bartky describes this work as "emotional caretaking" but could just as well have called it "interlocutory caretaking," since it is almost always the case that the service of emotional care is provided to a man through various communicative gestures that reinforce the importance and coherence of what he is saying. Bartky mentions, for example, the tendency of women to offer "a variety of verbal signals (sometimes called "conversational cheerleading") that incite him to continue speaking, hence reassuring him of the importance of what he is saying."[44] Bartky's argument echoes that made in a number of studies over the past few decades, studies that have shown women providing more "backchannel communication" to men than what men tend to provide them.[45] Backchannel responses (or what Bartky colloquially calls "conversational cheerleading") are those that serve to positively assess and reinforce what is being said by the other speaker. These can take a variety of short verbal forms — lexical and non-lexical (e.g., "uh-huh," "interesting," "I see," "hmm," "really?," "amazing," "that's terrible"). They can also include more substantive forms of reinforcement, such as asking for further elaboration or deliberately echoing the account just given in order to express agreement with it. Nonverbal gestures also provide an important form of interlocutory support. These gestures include not only nodding but a wide range of subtle ways of communicating empathy, such as "the compassionate squeezing of a hand" or "the sympathetic furrowing of a brow."[46]

Of course, it is important for us to have empathetic listeners, even "conversational cheerleaders." Authors like Jennifer Coates, Sara Mills, and Kathryn Scott[47] are thus right to point out that these habits of communication are not fundamentally disabling in themselves and that they serve an important role in maintaining the smooth functioning of a group's interactions. As I have been arguing throughout this book, the capacity to use language to interpret and reinterpret the world is of tremendous value, but, as we saw in the previous chapter, the exercise of this capacity hinges on knowing that there are others who will (or who at least might) listen to me. To participate in the disclosure of the world through speech requires me to believe there is some other for whom my speech or writing takes place. In the previous chapter, we explored this in terms of the importance of bearing witness to those who have undergone trauma, because their own capacity to develop an understanding of what they have undergone requires that others are willing to bear witness to what they have to say. Bartky too recognizes the importance of having an empathetic listener in one's life, someone who can nurture the accounts that we give of what we have experienced, seen, figured out, and so on. At the same time, she points out, that "here, as elsewhere, men's needs are not only likelier to be satisfied than women's needs but satisfied at women's expense."[48] The point, then, is not that all one-way channels of communication, in which one person backchannels for another, are bad. Indeed, this sort of interlocutory caretaking is vital for all of us to perform and receive at times. For Bartky, the problem emerges only at the point where a woman takes on so much of this caretaking work that her ability to actively engage in interpreting the world becomes diminished. Borrowing Marx's concept, Bartky refers to this situation as "alienation."[49]

By focusing on alienation, Bartky's understanding of the harm that can accompany emotional labor differs slightly from the account presented by Ferguson. While Ferguson understands the harm to lie specifically in the exploitation that occurs through the unequal exchange, that is, in how women provide more emotional labor than they receive, Bartky argues that the real harm lies in women surrendering their capacity to construct a worldview for themselves or, as she puts it, "the capacity, free from the subtle manipulation of consent, to construct an ethical and epistemic standpoint of one's own."[50] In the first chapter, I explained that there is a certain kind of empowerment that occurs when one develops into a linguistic being. As a linguistic being, the meaning of things and the ends to which I am directed are not just given to me to accept as is, but require me to engage in the task of interpretation. When I regularly direct my powers of world disclosure to serve as a backchannel for another, however, I am stunted in the development of this capacity. Like Marx, then, for whom the capacity of creative labor is essential to human fulfillment, Bartky understands alienation to consist not in the conscious awareness of being harmed or cheated, but in the diminishment of that capacity essential to human flourishing. Bartky reformulates Marx's concept of alienation, however, to focus not on the loss of creative labor in general but specifically on the loss of the creative labor of linguistic meaning-making—that capacity, for hermeneutic phenomenology, that is essential to human existence.

In the next chapter, we will have a chance to examine the consequences of becoming firmly entrenched in this form of alienation by looking at one specific communicative interaction in which the reduction of two-way communication to one-way communication is particularly detrimental, namely, the interaction between therapist and patient. Here again I will rely on feminist research on patterns in communication related to gender. In particular, I will draw from the clinical research of Julia Kristeva, an important figure in the Continental feminist tradition, as well as research by psychologist Dana Crowley Jack; both explore the relationship between women's communication patterns and depression. Although the term "depression" may be more ready-to-hand for us than the concept of alienation, I argue that the depression they describe is one that is intimately bound up with the habits of linguistic alienation that Bartky identifies.

Such linguistic alienation cannot be properly understood with a model of language that brackets out the influence of others on our speech, taking this kind of mediation as a violation of our linguistic authenticity. This model, which contemporary identity politics makes quite tempting, overlooks the essential role that others have in our own linguistic identification and risks rendering invisible the value of empathetic listening alongside other forms of interlocutory caregiving. To value such things does not mean turning a blind eye, however, to the problem of women's silence. We can both recognize responsivity as valuable for the linguistic being while taking seriously the harm that can result from overinvesting in such a role. To do this, I argue, we need a critical feminist perspective, one from which we both affirm that world disclosure is always a shared undertaking, but also give due attention to the power dynamics that can emerge within these social relations. In this chapter, I hope to have developed the contours of such a perspective by highlighting the productive points of overlap between feminist theory and philosophical hermeneutics. It is from this perspective that my analysis proceeds in the next chapter.

NOTES

1. Hans-Georg Gadamer, *Truth and Method*, trans. Joel Weinsheimer and Donald G. Marshall (London: Bloomsbury, 2004), 569.
2. Michaele L. Ferguson, "Sharing Without Knowing: Collective Identity in Feminist and Democratic Theory," *Hypatia* 22, no. 4 (2007): 30.

3. Georgia Warnke, "Race, Gender, and Antiessentialist Politics," *Signs: Journal of Women in Culture and Society* 31, no. 1 (2005): 93.

4. Dale Spender, *Man Made Language* (London: Routledge & Kegan Paul, 1980), 12; see also Mary Daly, *Gyn/Ecology: The Metaethics of Radical Feminism* (Boston: Beacon Press, 1978).

5. I am referring here to the Sapir-Whorf hypothesis that I presented in the book's introduction. For an account of the connection between this theory of language and feminist theory, see Michael J. Schneider and Karen A. Foss, "Thought, Sex, and Language: The Sapir-Whorf Hypothesis in the American Women's Movement," *Women's Studies in Communication* 1, no. 1 (1977): 1–7; and Deborah Cameron, *Feminism and Linguistic Theory* (London: Macmillan Press, 1992), 133.

6. Spender, *Man Made Language*, 2.

7. Significant landmarks in the development of Muted Group Theory and its application to women include Edwin Ardener, "Belief and the Problem of Women" and "The 'Problem' Revisited," in *Perceiving Women*, ed. Shirley Ardener (London: Malaby Press, 1975), 1–17 and 19–27; Shirley Ardener, *Defining Females: The Nature of Women in Society* (London: Croom Helm, 1978); and Cheris Kramarae, *Women and Men Speaking* (Rowley, MA: Newbury House, 1981).

8. Adrienne Rich, *The Dream of a Common Language: Poems 1974–1977* (New York: W. W. Norton, 1978), 16.

9. Deborah Cameron, for example, argues that the foundation of Rich's rhetoric can be found in Muted Group Theory. See Cameron, *Feminism and Linguistic Theory*, 130.

10. Héléne Cixous, "The Laugh of Medusa," in *The Women and Language Debate: A Sourcebook*, ed. Camille Roman, Suzanne Juhasz, and Cristanne Miller (New Brunswick, NJ: Rutgers University Press, 1994), 81.

11. Ibid., 80.

12. "The new history is coming; it's not a dream, though it does extend beyond men's imagination. . . . It is impossible to *define* a feminine practice of writing, and this is an impossibility that will remain, for this practice can never be theorized, enclosed, coded—which doesn't mean that it doesn't exist." Cixous, "The Laugh of Medusa," 84.

13. Ibid., 82.

14. It should be noted that Butler studied with Gadamer in 1979 during her year as a Fulbright Scholar in Heidelberg. Butler rarely mentions Gadamer in her writing, but, as I hope to show, her project carries forward important insights from the tradition of philosophical hermeneutics.

15. Judith Butler, "Imitation and Gender Subordination," in *Inside Out: Lesbian Theories, Gay Theories*, ed. Diana Fuss (New York: Routledge, 1991), 13–31.

16. Judith Butler, "Undiagnosing Gender," in *Undoing Gender* (New York: Routledge, 2004), 75–101.

17. Judith Butler, "Is Kinship Always Already Heterosexual?," in *Undoing Gender* (New York: Routledge, 2004), 102–30.

18. In *Gender Trouble*, Butler asks: "Is there a history of how the duality of sex was established, a genealogy that might expose the binary options as a variable construction? Are the ostensibly natural facts of sex discursively produced by various scientific discourses in the service of other political and social interests?" Judith Butler, *Gender Trouble: Feminism and the Subversion of Identity* (New York: Routledge, 1999), 10.

19. While I bring up these titles to illustrate some of the ways that we use categories of gender to interpret our lives, even in cases where the relevance of gender is unclear, I would be remiss if I did not also point out the role that such literature plays in mystifying the nature of women's subordination. These books and others like them mislead women about the nature of their struggles. Worst of all, they suggest that women are responsible for their struggles. Unfortunately, too many readers gravitate toward the solutions that they offer instead of consulting more systemic analyses.

20. See Helen E. Longino, *Science as Social Knowledge: Values and Objectivity in Scientific Inquiry* (Princeton, NJ: Princeton University Press, 1990); and Helen E. Longino, *The Fate of Knowledge* (Princeton, NJ: Princeton University Press, 2002).

21. In "On Truth and Lie in an Extra-Moral Sense," Nietzsche casts suspicion on the concept of truth by arguing that what we normally think of as being truthful amounts to no more than using conventional, agreed-upon terms to describe the world, and that this conventional usage provides us with nothing but illusions. "Truths," Nietzsche famously says, "are illusions about which one has forgotten that this is what they are." Friedrich Nietzsche, "On Truth and Lie in an Extra-Moral Sense," in *The Portable Nietzsche,* trans. and ed. Walter Kaufmann (New York: Penguin, 1982), 47.

22. Martin Heidegger, *Being and Time,* trans. John Macquarrie and Edward Robinson (New York: Harper & Row, 1962), 174. See my discussion of Heidegger's concept of *Geworfenheit* (thrownness) in chapter 1.

23. Gadamer, *Truth and Method,* 278–96; see also Hans-Georg Gadamer, "The Universality of the Hermeneutical Problem," in *Philosophical Hermeneutics,* trans. and ed. David E. Linge (Berkeley: University of California Press, 1977), 9.

24. Martin Heidegger, *On the Way to Language,* trans. Peter Hertz (New York: Harper & Row, 1971), 75. See my discussion of this theme in Heidegger's work in chapter 2.

25. Warnke finds a similar parallel between Butler and the hermeneutic tradition on this point. See Georgia Warnke, "Hermeneutics and Constructed Identities," in *Feminist Interpretations of Hans-Georg Gadamer,* ed. Lorraine Code (University Park: Pennsylvania State University Press, 2003), 72–73.

26. Butler develops this in part as a response to criticism received from Seyla Benhabib. See Seyla Benhabib, "Feminism and Postmodernism," in *Feminist Contentions: A Philosophical Exchange* (New York: Routledge, 1995), 17–34.

27. Judith Butler, *Giving an Account of Oneself* (New York: Fordham University Press, 2005), 24.

28. See Hans-Georg Gadamer, "To What Extent Does Language Preform Thought?" in *Truth and Method,* trans. Joel Weinsheimer and Donald G. Marshall (London: Bloomsbury, 2004), 568–75.

29. Emmanuel Levinas, *Totality and Infinity: An Essay on Exteriority,* trans. Alphonso Lingis (Pittsburgh, PA: Duquesne University Press, 1969), 194.

30. Ibid., 195.

31. Butler, *Giving an Account of Oneself,* 63.

32. Judith Butler, *Parting Ways: Jewishness and the Critique of Zionism* (New York: Columbia University Press, 2012), 24.

33. David Loy, *The World Is Made of Stories* (Somerville, MA: Wisdom Publications, 2010), 10.

34. Regarding the importance of both tasks in Butler's work, see Carolyn Culbertson, "The Ethics of Relationality: Judith Butler and Social Critique," *Continental Philosophy Review* 46, no. 3 (2013): 449–63.

35. These questions carry forward the project that Robin Pappas and William Cowling call "critical hermeneutics," which involves "extending Gadamerian hermeneutics to incorporate gendered, political, and social aspects of understanding." Robin Pappas and William Cowling, "Toward a Critical Hermeneutics," in *Feminist Interpretations of Hans-Georg Gadamer,* ed. Lorraine Code (University Park: Pennsylvania State University Press, 2003), 206.

36. Sandra Bartky, "Feeding Egos and Tending Wounds: Deference and Disaffection in Women's Emotional Labor," in *Femininity and Domination: Studies in the Phenomenology of Oppression* (New York: Routledge, 1990), 102.

37. Ibid., 119.

38. Ann Ferguson, *Blood at the Root: Motherhood, Sexuality, and Male Dominance* (London: Pandora, 1989).

39. See Karl Marx, *Capital: A Critique of Political Economy, Volume 1* (New York: International Publishers, 1967), 218.

40. See Carole Pateman, *The Sexual Contract* (Palo Alto, CA: Stanford University Press, 1988).

41. Bartky, *Femininity and Domination*, 100.

42. Ibid., 113.

43. Ibid., 113.

44. Ibid., 102.

45. For a summary of these studies, see Elizabeth Aries, *Men and Women in Interaction: Reconsidering the Differences* (Oxford: Oxford University Press, 1996). See also Judith A. Hall, Julie T. Irish, Debra L. Roter, Carol M. Ehrlich, and Lucy H. Miller, "Gender in Medical Encounters: An Analysis of Physician and Patient Communication in a Primary Care Setting," *Health Psychology* 13, no. 5 (1994): 384–92.

46. Bartky, *Femininity and Domination*, 103.

47. See Jennifer Coates, "Gossip Revisited: Language in All-Female Groups" in *Language and Gender: A Reader*, ed. Jennifer Coates and Pia Pichler (Malden, MA: Wiley-Blackwell, 2011), 199–223; Sara Mills, "Discourse Competence: Or How to Theorize Strong Women Speakers," *Hypatia: A Journal of Feminist Philosophy* 7, no. 2 (1992): 4–17; and Kathryn Scott, "Perceptions of Communication Competence: What's Good for the Goose is Not Good for the Gander," *Women's Studies International Quarterly* 3, no. 2 (1990): 199–208.

48. Bartky, *Femininity and Domination*, 113.

49. "This relation is the relation of the worker to his own activity as an alien activity not belonging to him; it is activity as suffering, strength as weakness, begetting as emasculating, the worker's *own* physical and mental energy, his personal life—for what is life but activity?—as an activity which is turned against him, independent of him and not belonging to him." Karl Marx, *Economic and Philosophical Manuscripts of 1844*, trans. Martin Milligan (Amherst, NY: Prometheus Books, 1988), 75.

50. Bartky, *Femininity and Domination*, 117.

FIVE

The Omnipotent Word of Medical Diagnosis and the Silence of Depression

On Kristeva's Therapeutic Approach

It is common today to think about depression as an illness best understood and thus best managed by medical specialists. Indeed, the medical language of depression increasingly gives people a way of signaling to others that what they suffer from needs no further elaboration—it is what it is: hormonal, genetic, a disease—words whose authority is all the more accepted the more they are interpreted by specialists. Such an approach to managing sadness has its appeal. Insofar as such diagnoses can help people manage symptoms that make their lives unlivable, there is great value in them. And insofar as people suffering from depression feel overwhelmed and not in control of their symptoms, it is natural to want to accept a medical diagnosis that lends the authority of science to that experience. Less obvious, however, is how the power of the verbal diagnosis itself can contribute to the therapeutic effect. The swift intervention of medical resources—hospitals, clinics, crisis centers, all with well-managed protocols and steady teams of dutiful professionals capable of dispensing wonder drugs—can provide a depressive person with a sense of great, albeit temporary relief, irrespective of the drugs' effects. For these reasons, despite studies that suggest the limited success of biomedical approaches to depression, many who struggle with depression are nevertheless receptive to the biomedical interpretation and treatment of their condition.[1]

Women constitute the majority of this group. Indeed, a recent study reports that one in four American women are currently using antidepressants, compared to 15 percent of American men.[2] This fact alone would seem to suggest that women who suffer from depression find value in the biomedical approach. What is appealing about this approach to patients in the throes of depression is, however, exactly what should give feminists pause: how silent the patient often is throughout the process of diagnosis and treatment.

This silence is not obvious from all interpretive standpoints. Indeed, authors like Kimberly K. Emmons are right to draw our attention to the veritable proliferation of talk about depression in recent years, especially talk guided by direct-to-consumer ads created by pharmaceutical companies about depression.[3] This silence comes clearly into view, however, when we examine the situation from the critical feminist standpoint developed in the previous chapter. This means acknowledging that the attachments women typically have to others take a different, more normalized, and thus often more intense form than the attachments men typically have. And while a critical feminist standpoint requires that we refrain from pathologizing these attachments, it also means recognizing, as Bartky's analysis from the previous chapter shows, that women's attachments to others take place today in a social context of inequality—a context in which they are encouraged to silence their own needs and concerns, and they often choose to remain silent rather than risk the negative consequences of speech.

This picture of women's silence has become clearer in light of recent studies spearheaded by feminist psychologist Dana Crowley Jack that demonstrate a direct correlation between depression and the tendency to silence the self. This tendency consists of a relational pattern in which a woman regularly judges herself based on external standards; puts the needs and desires of others above her own; inhibits self-expression and action in order to secure relationships and avoid conflict, retaliation, and loss; and, as a consequence, experiences being divided from herself.[4] The roots of these habits begin early in childhood, Jack suspects, when girls are encouraged more than boys to attach to their mothers and to seek reassurance and support from others. Later, a number of cultural norms will lead some women to adapt a strategy of self-silencing in an attempt to protect valued relationships that come into conflict with their own interests. Ignoring their own needs and silencing their own self-expression will seem like a viable strategy for women wishing to maintain the relationships they value in a society where women are expected to be self-sacrificing. Jack's findings show that habits of self-silencing not only tend to correlate with depression, a finding that has been replicated in numerous studies with women around the world, but also tend to make recovery more difficult.[5] This is because, when engrossed in these habits and in the kind of culture that fosters them, a woman is more likely to avoid expressing her grief to others and seeking social support for herself, which are vital to recovery.

From a critical feminist perspective, then, we ought to pay close attention to those women who struggle with depression and who—through isolation and self-silencing—withdraw in certain ways from verbal interaction and other crucial components of their linguistic being. To listen to women who withdraw in this way means paying attention to firsthand accounts of depression such as Maud Casey's; she writes, "Unfortunately to be depressed is not to have words to describe it, is not to have words at all, but to live in the gray world of the inarticulate, where nothing takes shape, nothing has edges or clarity."[6]

At the same time, occupying this feminist standpoint also requires us to consider how these habits are further enabled by the hierarchical interaction of common biomedical treatment, a connection that, at this point, has received very little scholarly attention.[7] Such habits predispose a woman to accept the interpretation of her doctors, whose authority is flanked by the symbolic prestige of their profession and the unique performative power wielded in their speech. After all, the doctor's diagnosis literally has the power of prescription.[8] Put into a prescription, it authorizes medication. Scribbled onto a note, it can excuse a patient from worldly obligations: job, school, and more. It prescribes how others in the crisis center or the hospital are to act around the individual. All of this contrasts with the patient's sense of her own language as something that never manages to work well, because she cannot communicate to others why and how she grieves. By contrast, the power of medical interpretation is great. Its performative magic is especially spectacular when its authority to prescribe action works within institutions where an individual is often without a powerful advocate, such as the prison or the courtroom. Such authoritative performative speech has the power to confront institutions that can otherwise appear omnipotent. Hence the appeal of the doctor's interpretation for a woman to whom language appears broken. With the doctor's diagnosis, she can remain silent. She has no need to venture into the realm of meaning-making, trying to bring to words exactly what stirs through her. The doctor authorizes her silence, gives it a name, and she only needs to utter this name.

The power of psychiatric language is evident in diagnosis and prescription alike. Just as medical diagnosis allows a woman suffering from unspeakable emptiness to remain within the affective field of the body, withdrawn from the linguistic process, the drugs she is prescribed do as well. The authority of the doctor's speech is transmitted metonymically into the drugs she accepts, giving them special meaning.[9] Her acceptance, more than likely, is a rather silent one. She accepts the drugs orally—using her mouth to ingest the doctor's speech. If it is also verbal, that is, if she agrees to the treatment, it is not likely to be a long deliberation, as oral ingestion is psychologically easier for her than conversation. She remains withdrawn from speech until the end of the depressive episode's duration, until she feels stable enough again to return to her normal

worldly affairs. She leaves without actively contributing to the interpretation of her condition, protected from the pain of interaction that soothes
her such that, along with the medication, her disposition is temporarily
improved. If the doctor prescribes a regimen of counseling as aftercare,
she is likely to accept the doctor's suggestion but not likely to show up
for those talking sessions.[10] What is there really to say? All of this talk
won't do anything. Nobody gets it, but the drugs help her to survive.

Undoubtedly there are times when immediate survival requires putting trust in medical authorities. In this chapter, however, I argue that in
the many cases of female depression in which isolation and self-silencing
have contributed to the collapse of linguistic meaning, there is good reason to believe that a strategy for long-term healing must include, rather
than avoid, rehabilitating the depressive person's capacity for meaningful speech. Carrying forward insights developed in the previous two
chapters, I argue that doing so requires the patient to participate actively
in interpreting her own experience—an achievement not accomplished
by the patient in isolation but with the assistance of an empathetic listener. Here I will draw from an analysis of depression offered by another
leading Continental feminist thinker—Julia Kristeva, in her 1987 study,
Black Sun: Depression and Melancholia. After presenting Kristeva's explanation of why depression is often accompanied by a withdrawal from language, and bringing Kristeva's theory into conversation with Jack's model of self-silencing, I will describe how Kristeva's therapeutic approach
offers a more effective way of helping women who are suffering in silence than the diagnosis-based medical model can offer.

My aim in this chapter, then, is to contribute further to an understanding of the suffering caused by linguistic alienation—in this case, linguistic
alienation accompanying depression—and to an understanding of the
conditions that enable those suffering in this way to heal. Along the way,
though, I also hope to shed light on what drives so many women to
accept the word of medical diagnosis as omnipotent, and why this acceptance is nevertheless uncertain for some. It may seem as though the first
question of what drives people toward diagnosis has already been sufficiently addressed in the literature. Indeed, we now have several compelling explanations of the cultural and symbolic power of psychiatric discourse, including notably that explanation offered by Michel Foucault in
Madness and Civilization. Foucault provides us with a genealogical account of how psychiatric discourse has come to speak the truth of human
sadness, that is, how it has developed the sovereign authority to represent and analyze sadness, to tell us what it is, how it works, and what to
do about it. Foucault even speaks about this as a kind of silencing that
takes place when the psychiatric discourse on mental illness in general
becomes the privileged episteme. He writes:

> In the serene world of mental illness, modern man no longer communicates with the madman: on the one hand, the man of reason delegates the physician to madness, thereby authorizing a relation only through the abstract universalization of disease; on the other hand, the man of madness communicates with society only by the intermediary of an equally abstract reason. . . . As for common language, there is no such thing; or rather, there is no such thing any longer. . . . The language of psychiatry, which is a monologue of reason about madness, has been established only on the basis of such a silence. [11]

Foucault's genealogical account suggests that it is the representational power of psychiatric discourse that compels people to seek and accept diagnoses. What his account does not explain, however, is what it is about rationalizing representation in itself that is desirable, nor does it address the ambivalent, alienated relationship that many people—particularly those women stuck in the cycle of self-silencing—have toward this rationalizing representation. In fact, Foucault cannot address this ambivalence if he holds onto the strong claim that a person's experience of suffering has always been perfectly accounted for by—that is, abstractly universalized by—psychiatric discourse. By contrast, Kristeva's work sheds important light on why people, particularly women, desire representation for their suffering in the first place such that the cultural significance of diagnosis is appealing and, more to the point, on why the desire some have for this representation is conflicted and self-defeating. Because such considerations are anterior to answering the question of what healing depression requires, I develop them at length in what follows before returning to the question of healing.

KRISTEVA'S ACCOUNT OF SILENCE IN DEPRESSION

As I have suggested, those who have adopted habits of self-silencing often welcome medical diagnosis and prescription, not only because of the practical benefits to having such authority on their side but because, in their seemingly univocal power, these forms of speech allow them to remain silent and to avoid participating in linguistic expression. But rather than accounting for this phenomenon entirely through an analysis of the symbolic power of biomedical discourse, what we need, I have suggested, is a deeper look at what makes some people, particularly women, receptive to such authoritative discourse to begin with. This is something that Continental feminist philosophy, particularly psychoanalytic feminist theory, can shed light on. To answer this question, then, I would like to turn to Kristeva's *Black Sun* and, in particular, the explanation it offers as to what sustains habits of self-silencing, what Kristeva describes as a "withdrawal from language."

Like other psychoanalysts, Kristeva recognizes that the roots of a depression reach deeper than the particular loss that triggers it, for example, the death of a loved one, a betrayal, or a setback at work. As Freud
observes in "Mourning and Melancholia," whereas in mourning one can
easily name the source of one's grief, the melancholic person appears to
suffer from something ineffable, that is, a loss she cannot name. Indeed,
Freud explains, even the physician has a hard time articulating what is
lost. He states: "One cannot see clearly what it is that has been lost, and it
is all the more reasonable to suppose that the patient cannot consciously
perceive what he has lost either." [12] Seen only in this light, then, depression can be bewildering to some, who rightly observe that the force with
which depression takes over a person's life is disproportionate to the
trigger itself. Such disproportion can even be an important criterion for
diagnosing depression according to the current *Diagnostic and Statistical
Manual of Mental Disorders (DSM-V)*. [13]

Now, the fact that depression is disproportionate to any trigger leads
many nonspecialists to conclude that the cause of a depression is ultimately internal and subjective, that it is "all in the head." And in a culture
that views women as the more fragile, sensitive sex, the fact that women
experience depression twice as much as men seems to lend support to
this popular view of depression. [14] But when we start to pay attention to
the patterns of self-silencing, this popular view runs into problems on a
couple of points. First, it ignores external causes that may be long in the
making, along with the vicious cycle that such external causes may have
set in motion. But a depressive response can become so exacerbated by
feelings of low self-regard and impulses toward isolation that whatever
initially precipitated the reaction seems quite insignificant compared to
dealing with its effects. Second, this popular view that depression is "all
in the head" describes as an entirely *internal* tendency of women, something that women have likely developed as a response to external factors.
In other words, if women are twice as likely to experience depression,
then, rather than assuming that it is something in women's nature that
leads to depression, we ought to see if there are things happening to
women that lead them to routinely develop this "internal" landscape. On
both points, Kristeva's account of depression is insightful. It sheds light
on how silence can exacerbate suffering to a point that it overshadows the
original cause, and—when interpreted alongside Jack's theory of self-
silencing—accounts for the high rate of depression in women without
attributing causality to a woman's "nature," which is more than likely the
effect and not the cause of cultural stereotypes.

Rather than taking the source to be internal, Kristeva understands
depression as a compromise formation that develops in an attempt to
deal with loss. While a number of emotional setbacks can trigger depression, Kristeva argues that the force of these setbacks can be traced back to
another deeper, ongoing loss, what she calls the loss of the "archaic pre-

object." Here we reach a rather technical point in Kristeva's discussion; however, while the use of a term like "archaic preobject" may deter some readers, it will be helpful for our purposes to parse its meaning, as it is central to Kristeva's account of the linguistic being and its vulnerability to depression. For Kristeva, the loss of the archaic preobject has two distinct but related senses, both of which bespeak the importance that psychoanalysis places on childhood experiences for psychical development. First, it is the ongoing loss of the infant being's narcissism, a time that is *preobjectal* in that it precedes any awareness of the distinction between subject and object. In early narcissism, one does not see that the world is a world for others, too, as one does not yet know any real lack or limitation, is not yet self-conscious. To experience an external world that is not me, however, even if it is a necessary and vital insight, is a blow to the early narcissistic self. It marks the loss of the preobjectal state of being, the wounds of which can continue to throb throughout even adult life. Second, Kristeva describes this ongoing loss as a loss of a certain relationship to the mother. The mother is set up as the preobject as the infant being "clings to another, perceives it as a supplement, artificial extension, protective wrapping,"[15] that is, at a time of utter vulnerability, when the infant requires the protection of another being from whom it cannot yet distinguish itself. Putting these two together, the loss of the preobject, then, is the loss of that mode of being that preexists a world of subjects and objects, a world structured by an awareness of my separation from others. In sum, in order to understand oneself as an individuated subject, Kristeva argues, one must undergo a difficult transition away from two things: away from an early narcissism upset by self-consciousness, and away from an attachment to the mother as preobject. Following Freud, Kristeva calls this transition the negation [*Verneinung*] of loss.

For Kristeva, the negation of the loss of the archaic preobject is necessary, not only because of a cultural emphasis on individuated subjectivity and not only within the history of sexual contract and heterosexual family relations (where I am forbidden to keep my mother as my love object), but also as a necessary feature of any life wherein meaning is set forth between people through language. This is because meaning requires a transformation away from the infant mode of being for which no other exists. It requires that one inhabit the world as a linguistic being, so that meaning is found not in the immediacy of things but in the participatory process of world disclosure.[16] This development, from immediacy to linguistic mediation, is not only a part of the subject's development of self-awareness but is also vital to her development as a communicator. Echoing the importance placed on the role of non-immediacy in the linguistic world that we explored in chapter 2, Kristeva describes this as the abyss or break necessary for speech. She writes:

> Our gift of speech, of situating ourselves in time for another, could
> exist nowhere except beyond an abyss. Speaking beings, from their
> ability to endure in time up to their enthusiastic, learned, or simply
> amusing constructions, demand a break, a renunciation, an unease at
> their foundations. The negation of that fundamental loss opens up the
> realm of signs for us.[17]

On this account, then, it is not just a particular historical culture that
requires one to cope with the loss of the archaic preobject, but the development of the linguistic mode of being itself.

Into what, then, do we transfer our erotic investment when we grow
away from the infant union with the preobject? Here again the answer
has two parts, reflecting the two accounts of psychical development that
Kristeva takes up from Freudian psychoanalysis. First, Kristeva answers
that a person must transfer some erotic investment from the mother onto
a new object of affection. This can take the form of affection toward and
identification with an ideology or a group, but in most cases it will also
mean affection toward another person.[18]

Second, and more significant for our purposes, a person copes with
the loss through a process of linguistic identification, becoming someone
for whom meaning (including one's own meaning) is found in the adven-
ture of linguistic world disclosure and not just in the immediate plenti-
tude of preobject life. Here Kristeva's conception of how one might
manage to cope with the loss mirrors the account given in chapter 3 about
how language functions in recovery from trauma. In both cases, linguistic
identification becomes a means of coping with a loss that is otherwise
unbearable by transforming or "negating" it. Having suffered the loss,
linguistic identification enables the psyche to live on, assuring itself: "I
have lost an essential object that happens to be, in the final analysis, my
mother. . . . But no, I have found her again in signs, or rather since I
consent to lose her I have not lost her (that is the negation), I can recover
her in language."[19]

In arguing that linguistic identification "ensures the subject's entrance
into the universe of signs and creation" and, in so doing, enables a "triumph over sadness," Kristeva's own position is consistent with that of
her psychoanalytic predecessors—both Freud and Jacques Lacan.[20] At
the same time, Kristeva is much more sensitive to how precarious this
process of linguistic identification can be. Indeed, Kristeva parts ways
from her psychoanalytic predecessors in insisting that the negation of
loss, the transformation away from our initial attachments, is never complete. This is why she insists, contrary to Freud, that there is no sharp
distinction between mourning and melancholy. For her, all mourning
(i.e., negation of loss) must include a kernel of melancholy (i.e., attachment to the archaic preobject). All meaning remains bound up with a
loss—"a break, a renunciation, an unease at [our] foundations."[21] In the
context of linguistic identification, then, this means that we never manage

to completely recover the prelinguistic mode of being as an object of our own consent. Such attempts to "triumph" once and for all over loss are self-defeating. One will always need to negotiate between being relationally constituted as a subject and realizing from time to time that the other's needs and desires are not one's own, that one's own needs and desires are not hers. At times, this process will feel like loss. For Kristeva, however, as we shall see, the survival of the subject requires that one bear this loss so that new experiences of meaning—linguistic and interpersonal—can be opened up.

WOMEN'S SILENCE AND ITS CONSEQUENCES FOR DEPRESSION

As we have just seen, Kristeva argues that all of us must undergo a labor of mourning to some extent as part of the normal development of subjectivity, since the subject must always reckon with its relational constitution. Yet, as the previous two chapters have made clear, a number of contingent social circumstances make participating in language more difficult for some than others. These are social circumstances beyond a person's control that help or hinder their effort to "triumph over sadness," that is, to negate loss through linguistic identification. Though Kristeva fails to develop this point in her work, it is an important one, particularly for understanding the gendered dimension of depression. After all, in identifying myself as an object in language, I am constrained by the terms that are available to me and thus "I" will wax and wane with the flux of symbolic authority enjoyed by those terms of identity I choose. I may undergo the process of linguistic identification much more seamlessly if I can be made to fit easily into a set of identity categories popularly in use in my culture (i.e., terms that allow me to easily claim for myself some professional identity, gender identity, familial role, or political ideology) and if I can express myself fluently in the language(s) available to me. Moreover, as discussed in the previous chapter, such norms will tend to be gendered, meaning that I can triumph in linguistic identification if and only if I undergo a process of gendering—a process that is both formative and constraining.[22] Thus, I remain dependent on others even as a speaking being, just as I was in infancy. I cannot self-diagnose if there is no convention of self-diagnosis. Likewise, I will not express frustration or pain if there is nobody who will listen to me, recognizing me as a meaningful source of world disclosure, or if I fear retaliation for speaking. The point is that this process of negation (the negation of the loss of the archaic preobject) is not simply the triumph of some individual mind, indifferent to social constraints. Its success hinges on precisely the kinds of social enabling conditions that we have been exploring in recent chapters. If our words are to have power, we must still cling to others, not unlike the infant clinging to its mother.

While Kristeva does not sufficiently examine the way that circumstances like these can foster or hinder linguistic identification, she is more
perceptive when it comes to other ways that gender bears on a person's
ability to negotiate loss through linguistic identification. Throughout her
work, Kristeva has explored the particular struggle that females tend to
have with this process of loss. They struggle, she believes, because, in
trying to negate the loss of the mother in the way described above, they
end up trying to negate aspects of feminine identity they typically possess. So, to the extent that a person identifies as female, she will continue
to be what she feels she is expected to develop beyond and, in a hetero-
normative culture, she will continue to love what she is not supposed to
love. As Kelly Oliver puts it: "Whereas the son splits the mother in order
to unify himself, if the daughter splits the mother she splits herself."[23] To
the degree that she cannot manage this paradoxical demand successfully,
a woman who has learned to defer to the needs of others will give her
own life in order to let the archaic preobject live on. In comparison with
what she perceives has been lost—this ineffable, archaic bond—language
will seem false and meaningless.

As we have just seen, drawing from Kristeva's account of depression
allows us to recognize how gender, a factor largely beyond the control of
an individual's attitude and irreducible to an object of consent, contrib-
utes to a person's propensity for depression. Jack's theory of self-silencing, however, sheds further light on the cultural forces that hinder
women's speaking, blocking them from processes of recovery through
linguistic meaning-making. In a recent volume that demonstrates the existence of this correlation in diverse cultures around the globe, Jack and
Ali explain how, for many women around the world, habits of self-silencing lead to depression. "When followed," they write, "these self-silencing
relational schemas create a vulnerability to depression by directing wom-
en to defer to the needs of others, censor self-expression, repress anger,
inhibit self-directed action, and judge the self against a culturally defined
'good woman.'"[24] Psychologist Laura S. Brown recognizes the role that
these relational schemas played in her own mother's struggle with depression decades ago. Brown explains that her own mother tended not to
give herself permission "to take the time and money that she needed to
heal emotionally, with 'selfish' being one of the worst epithets that could
be hurled at a woman in that era." She adds: "Silencing the self in favor of
what were constructed in the social narrative as the more valued, and
allegedly conflicting, needs of her family, was the order of the day for my
mother and other women like her."[25]

Although it emerges as a defense strategy intended to avoid painful
conflict, self-silencing behavior eventually takes its toll on a woman's life.
Indeed, the consequences of living with these habits become so dire that
they tend to eventually overshadow whatever initially triggered the need
for these defenses. David Karp makes a similar point about the uninten-

tional effects of isolation as a response to emotional setbacks. In *Speaking of Sadness*, he writes:

> Immediately, the urge to withdraw, to be alone, seems sensible when "it hurts even to talk," as one person described the difficulty of interaction. However, withdrawal turns out to be a false emotional economy. Although providing emotional respite from social obligations that seem impossible to carry out, withdrawal's long term effects are negative. Like drugs that have good short term effects and debilitating long term consequences, social withdrawal becomes part of a crucible melding fear and self-loathing, a brew that powerfully catalyzes hopelessness. Hopelessness, in turn, makes the urge to withdraw even more powerful. And so it goes—a truly vicious cycle. [26]

What Karp describes here goes for all self-silencing behavior, any form of which inevitably exacerbates the pain of an emotional setback, allowing that pain to spiral viciously out of hand, catalyzing hopelessness as one grows more and more mute. And, above all, this is because such behavior blocks the way to recovery through interpersonal linguistic meaning-making that is essential to healing. In light of this, we can return to our earlier discussion of the disproportionality of depression relative to any trigger. While in the face of this disproportionality it is common to hear non-specialists say that depression is "all in the head," the account I have given here instead suggests that the struggle a person has mourning loss or overcoming emotional setbacks cannot be traced back to her own purely internal agency, because being an active meaning-maker depends on a number of conditions that are not up to that person—notably, social circumstances affecting the efficacy of her speech and the likelihood that she will give voice to her suffering. Thus, it is clear that the transition that Kristeva describes away from ineffable loss and into the life of language is much farther out of reach for some than it is for others.

Women regularly struggle with this transition because of a number of social conditions that encourage them to stay silent. In the previous chapter, we explored the cultural expectation that women take on a disproportionate share of emotional caretaking, acting as empathetic listeners without receiving adequate emotional care in return. On top of this, socioeconomic patterns of caretaking encourage women to stay home, where they typically have few interactions with others outside of the family. We should also consider here the idealization of the selfless mother, who always puts the needs of her family before her own—a role prominent in many cultures and that tends to be formative for the sense of self that women who are stay-at-home mothers develop. Studies have suggested that such circumstances correlate with depression in women, [27] allowing women to slide even more deeply into self-silencing, into even that "gray world of the inarticulate" that Maud Casey describes. As Kristeva puts it:

"In the best of cases, speaking beings and their language are like one: is not speech our 'second nature'? In contrast, the speech of the depressed is to them like an alien skin; melancholy persons are foreigners in their maternal tongue. They have lost the meaning—the value—of their mother tongue for want of losing the mother." [28]

It is no wonder, then, that silence is often a prominent feature of depression. Emil Kraepelin, a contemporary of Freud, noticed this when he observed that those who are depressed "do not give information on their own initiative," and when they do, their speech is "mostly low, monotonous, hesitating, even stuttering," their writing "often indistinct and sprawling." [29] Such a withdrawal from language presents a problem for the work of psychoanalysis, which, of course, requires the patient to open up through speech and to respond to the speech of another. According to an interview written after her book was published, Kristeva says that it was this problem that most motivated her work in *Black Sun*. The problem, as she puts it, is that "if the depressed person rejects language and finds it meaningless or false, how can we gain access to his pain through speech, since psychoanalysts work with speech?" [30] Kristeva goes on to explain that she considers the strategy she developed as a response to this problem her greatest contribution to "the way psychoanalysts listen to depression." [31] Such listening will, as it turns out, require a particular kind of speech from the analyst herself. We turn now to examine what such a strategy of listening entails and how it differs from the way that a medical diagnosis engages a patient.

KRISTEVA'S THERAPEUTIC APPROACH: LISTENING TO THE DISCOURSE OF THE DEPRESSED

Earlier I described how, for Kristeva, there is no mourning that completely overcomes its attachment to what is lost. She resists Freud's distinction between mourning and melancholy, preferring to view mourning as an ongoing process of linguistic meaning-making that is never fully complete, never completely triumphant. In this way, the "negation" that Kristeva deems vital to healing is not a simple renunciation of prelinguistic life. Kristeva's approach to interacting with depressed patients reflects this understanding. At the basis of her therapeutic strategy lies the observation that, although people who are depressed often appear withdrawn from language and meaning-making, their symptom formations nevertheless offer a kind of discourse that can be read and that is potentially meaningful to them and others. Yet, based on what we have seen so far, we know that this language can only be meaningful when set forth in a way that does not force it to assert itself autonomously, essentially denying the infant's clinging condition. Two things are required to avoid this result. First of all, there must be an empathetic listener who attempts to identify with the expression of the symptoms. In *Black Sun*, this other is an analyst but not an anonymous, distant observer or experimenter. As Kristeva says in her later book, *Intimate Revolt*: "With depression, more than in any other analytical situation, the analyst is solicited to mobilize (the patient's) listening, (the patient's) unconscious, in an intense identification with the patient."[32] Next, to help the patient interpret her own condition, Kristeva explains that the analyst must look for an encrypted form of expression at work in the patient's affective display. She explains that, with people suffering from depression, their speech is "a mask—a beautiful façade carved out of a 'foreign language.' Nevertheless, if depressive speech avoids sentential signification, its meaning has not completely run dry. It occasionally hides . . . in the tone of the voice, which one must learn to understand in order to decipher the meaning of affect."[33]

To illustrate the point, Kristeva describes her experience with one patient, a woman named Anne, a professional anthropologist who suffered from frequent bouts of extreme sadness and withdrawal from meaningful activities. Despite her ability to function quite normally, even successfully in her career and in her social circle, Anne would frequently experience major depressive episodes where she would feel utterly disconnected from all of these projects. Kristeva reports that, after meeting with Anne several times and talking with her, she began to have the impression that the verbal exchange between them was merely leading to a rationalization of the symptoms, but not a working through. When Kristeva asked her about this, Anne confirmed to her that she felt she spoke "at the edge of (her) words," while the "bottom of (her) sorrow" remained "unreachable."[34] Anne was therefore able to function in the session, exchanging words, but experienced these words as futile in reaching the depths of her sorrow. Kristeva explains:

> I could have interpreted those words as a hysterical refusal of the castrating exchange with me. The interpretation, however, did not seem sufficient, considering the intensity of the depressive complaint and the extent of the silence that either settled in or broke up her speech in "poetic" fashion, making it, at times, undecipherable. I said, "At the edge of words, but at the heart of the voice, for your voice is uneasy when you talk about the incommunicable sadness."[35]

In recognizing the intensity of meaning in the woman's affect, Kristeva allows the patient herself to participate in how her sadness is articulated. While the patient cannot express her sadness in words, Kristeva finds that she nevertheless expresses her loss in other ways. Not only in the voice but, if we were to look through the entire case study, we would find also in her body language and even in the clothing she wears. All of these suggest to Kristeva the beginnings of an interpretation that Anne herself is giving to her own depression. Kristeva's task as an analyst is to recognize the potential meaning of these clues and, with them, to initiate a dialogue, bringing them into verbal expression.

These clues are found in the affective dimension of Anne's speech. This observation is important for understanding both what is happening in depression and how healing can take place. For we see that, first of all, instead of accepting symbolic language as compensation for loss, the depressed person clings to an affective display for meaning. It is the affective display that is cultivated in lieu of a bond to signifying language. In this way, the heavy feeling of sadness is actually functioning as a kind of substitute, a new object of attachment that arises in exchange for what is lost.[36] Because of this attachment, no offering of symbolic representation alone will suffice as a therapeutic method. Rather, the person must be engaged at another level where a meaningful expression of suffering is already beginning to unfold.

As the later chapters of *Black Sun* illustrate, we can find a similar expression of loss underway in some works of art, such as Hans Holbein's *The Body of the Dead Christ in the Tomb*. In works like this, Kristeva believes, we find precisely that mediation of loss underway in the depressive condition: an imaginary synthesis of representation and the unrepresentable void. As Kristeva later wrote, one finds in these forms of the imaginary "recognition of the right to pain."[37] Such recognition functions not as an antidepressant, but as a "counter-depressant," Kristeva says, steering one away from absolute attachment to the inexpressible preobject and a long-term withdrawal from language by engaging the discourse of depression on its own terms. Kristeva's approach to listening to the discourse of the depressed takes its cue from art in this way. Like the interpretation of the analyst, these "counter-depressants" can help bring inexpressible loss into the realm of expression by offering a person a way of actually mourning rather than relinquishing all attachment to the archaic preobject, setting forth "a device whose prosodic economy, interaction of characters, and implicit symbolism constitute a very faithful semiological representation of the subject's battle with symbolic collapse."[38]

But just as the synthesis underway in the artistic process must finally be externalized and objectified in a work, one that can be recognized by others as an expression of suffering, so too must the one quietly representing her loss through silent affect eventually externalize this process and share it with another. Otherwise, this effort to express loss can be deadly, for, as Kristeva describes, the desire for suicide emerges when one is overcome with longing for unification with the silence that now lives in the place of the lost object. So, while it is a necessary ingredient for effectively surviving deep loss, the interpretation of this wound that is underway in the affective display of depression is not enough by itself to prevent self-inflicted death. This is why Kristeva insists on transposition into the sphere of interpersonal, linguistic meaning-making. But again, this does not mean that cultural and linguistic representation are superimposed onto the meanings generated by the imaginary, but that the imaginary must be genuinely integrated into the symbolic. Sara Beardsworth takes this point to be essential to Kristeva's argument in *Black Sun*. As Beardsworth puts it: "The central thesis for Kristeva's account of melancholy is, therefore, the necessity of a symbolic form-giving that integrates the most archaic, or primitive, recording of loss/emptiness within the symbolic field: culture and language. Put otherwise, the imaginary is a necessary component of culture."[39] Necessary, that is, if culture is to be meaningful and livable.

For Kristeva, then, the cointerpretation of painful affect that takes place in analysis offers a way of effectively mourning rather than simply relinquishing all attachment to the archaic preobject, that formative relational bond. This healing technique, as we have seen, takes its lead not just from the clues that patients themselves provide about the meaning of their suffering but from the therapeutic potential of artworks that represent suffering in a way that symbolic representation cannot, resisting in the end any final, ultimate compensation for the loss they represent. The balance between these two poles—between speaking and silence, meaning and loss—is a difficult one, of course. And, as we have seen, it is easy to get pulled completely to one side or the other, as those who fall into habits of self-silencing know. But, on Kristeva's account, it is no less than meaning itself—and, in particular, our ability to find meaning as relational and linguistic beings—that is at stake in this balance.

A CRITICAL PERSPECTIVE ON DIAGNOSTIC SPEECH

Having traced out what, according to Kristeva and the literature on self-silencing, leads some women to withdraw from linguistic, interpersonal meaning and to cling to the silence of depressive affect, and having described Kristeva's own therapeutic strategy for recognizing and healing this suffering, let us now consider the effects of Kristeva's strategy alongside those of medical diagnosis, as previously discussed. In particular, we must examine how speech works in each case—whether it reinforces the withdrawal from language and meaning-making that occurs in self-silencing or, instead, encourages a new enterprise in interpersonal communication. To be clear, in drawing this comparison, I do not mean to suggest that all practitioners who engage in diagnostic and prescriptive speech rely exclusively on diagnosis to understand their patients' suffering, eschewing other forms of interaction. There has been, however, a clear shift in recent decades toward diagnosis and pharmaceutical treatment and away from psychotherapeutic approaches like Kristeva's that focus on long, in-depth dialogue.[40] In light of this shift, there are three important points of comparison that must be made.

First, in Kristeva's strategy, the analyst's words lack omnipotent, illocutionary power. They do not automatically accomplish an effect in their utterance.[41] In fact, they fail unless the patient herself verifies them by responding to them. The analyst aims only at opening up a path of self-interpretation for the patient herself, one that arises immanently through the communicative exchange. In implicating the patient into the meaning-making process, then, the patient must do more than consume the words. She must participate in the linguistic process of world disclosure. By contrast, the speech of diagnosis and prescription requires no recognition on the part of the person diagnosed nor, for that matter, any self-interpretation. It locates the meaning of the patient's symptoms in a referential world that is already established (a certain page in the *DSM-V*, for example), and thus gives the patient no drive to try and bring the intense affectivity of her sadness into words. That is, it does nothing to counteract the legacy of self-silencing that many women carry around with them. But the process of self-expression is, as we have seen, necessary for healing from depression—even if difficult for many women.

This brings me to the second point of comparison. While the omnipotent speech of diagnosis positions the physician as a separate, idealized other, the relationship with the analyst is much more intimate. This is important because an idealized other will function as a mere substitute for the lost preobject, another object of unmitigated attachment. To interact with an idealized other, then, cannot help a woman learn to negotiate between her deep relationality and her separateness from others. In Lacanian terms, such an interaction arrests desire, the life and the elaboration of which is ongoing.[42] Meanwhile, one certainly can desire to interpret their suffering for an empathetic listener. Indeed, this kind of interlocutor stirs up the desire for speech. And this is why, for Kristeva, the analyst must empathize and identify with the patient—engaging in what psychoanalysts call "counter-transference"—in order for the patient to relate to her own speech anew. As Kristeva puts it in *Intimate Revolt*, "The language of the depressed person, until now felt as emptiness because cut off from affective and vocal inscriptions, is revitalized in and through this interpretation and can become a space of desire, that is, meaning for the subject."[43] In comparison, diagnostic and prescriptive speech does not leave the speech of the one diagnosed charged with desire and meaning.

Third, we have seen that Kristeva's therapeutic strategy encourages a genuine synthesis of sorrowful affect and symbolic representation. It does this not through subsuming the former entirely into the latter, but by offering what Kristeva calls "recognition of the right to pain." Diagnostic and prescriptive speech, however, do not offer such reconciliation. As Foucault explains in the passage presented above from *Madness and Civilization*, the physician's diagnostic speech functions as the rationalization and the abstract universalization of psychical suffering because of its symbolic power. It thus assigns a name to what resists articulation, what—particularly in cases of self-silencing—clings to ineffability. But the effects of foregoing real reconciliation can be dire, for the demand to identify with diagnosis can require such an act of assertion over the primary drives that many people, when they are wounded by or afraid of loss, will instead cling fiercely to the mood of sadness instead of working through the experience with others. For them, it will be easier to swallow pills than to speak about their suffering. Being deprived of expression, silence remains the last connection they have with that archaic loss.

What ought we to take away from this comparison then? In this chapter, I have tried to show why some people find it especially difficult to work through suffering and loss through verbal interaction, why it is that many people—particularly women—are more comfortable staying silent than venturing into the linguistic activity of world disclosure. We have also seen that such a disposition often leads to and greatly exacerbates depression. For this reason, it is important for clinicians and anyone offering support to people in a depressive condition to be aware of what kind of verbal interaction tends to foster these patterns and what interaction will challenge them. But this problem is not always evident to those in this supportive role. It is easy, after all, to confuse the resignation of one's own meaning-making capacities for genuine consent through verbal interaction. After all, one's acceptance of diagnostic interpellation would seem to indicate that she has embraced that self-understanding, finding genuine self-expression in it. This is not to say that we should abandon the use of diagnoses completely but, rather, that those in supportive roles, particularly clinicians, ought to maintain a critical perspective on the kind of meaning that diagnostic speech provides to those who are depressed. We must check to see whether such speech is actually offering the person a way to reconcile with loss and to find meaning or not, and this requires turning a critical eye toward habits of verbal interaction that are often taken for granted in the medical world today. It also means paying great attention to silence, in the way that Kristeva does with her patient, Anne, understanding what a patient wants to say about her life in remaining quiet. Cultivating such a critical perspective in the care that we give will not single-handedly cure or prevent depression. But, I believe, it is an important part of making loss and pain livable.

To conclude, in light of the tendency of depressed persons, especially women, to detach from the process of interpersonal meaning-making as they suffer, we can see that there is much to recommend about Kristeva's therapeutic strategy. By contrast, while medical diagnosis and the actions it enables are certainly necessary at times when a person is in crisis, there is good reason to worry about the way medical diagnosis leaves a woman struggling with inexpressible sadness out of the process of interpretation, assigning a name to her suffering in a way that allows her to stay silent. The task that this comparison sets before us, though, is not an easy one. In the interest of long-term healing, it suggests that we allow ourselves to feel more vulnerable and to linger in the pain of loss, patiently undertaking the labor of its expression, something modern Western cultures, in their obsession with strength, productivity, and efficiency, grow increasingly unaccustomed to. Moreover, as Kristeva's work suggests, the challenge of helping each other through this process will not be met by a strategy of nonintervention, by simply striking out diagnostic discourse and expecting those now suffering in silence to suddenly speak for themselves in its place. Instead, interventions are needed to open up a space where people desire to give creative, intimate expression to their suffering. For in that activity of expression, sadness becomes livable.

NOTES

1. Recent placebo studies have suggested that pharmaceutical antidepressants by themselves are not effective treatments for depression. For a discussion of these findings, see Allan V. Horwitz and Jerome C. Wakefield, *The Loss of Sadness: How Psychiatry Transformed Normal Sorrow into Depressive Disorder* (Oxford: Oxford University Press, 2007), 191; and Richard Gordon's "Drugs Don't Talk: Do Medication and Biological Psychiatry Contribute to Silencing the Self?" in *Silencing the Self Across Cultures: Depression and Gender in the Social World*, ed. Dana Crowley Jack and Alisha Ali (Oxford: Oxford University Press, 2010), 55–56.

2. A Huffington Post article by Katherine Bindley, "Women and Prescription Drugs: One in Four Takes Mental Health Drugs" (https://www.huffingtonpost.com/2011/11/16/women-and-prescription-drug-use_n_1098023.html), describes the gender disparity uncovered by a 2011 Medco Health Solutions report based on claims data from 2.5 million Americans over the previous decade. Linda Blum and Nena Stracuzzi analyze the significance of this disparity in their article "Gender and the Prozac Nation: Popular Discourse and Productive Femininity," *Gender and Society* 18, no. 3 (2004): 269–86. Blum and Stracuzzi point out that, at that time, 67 to 80 percent of Prozac users were women, and that women were in general twice as likely to use psychotropics as men.

3. Kimberly K. Emmons, *Black Dogs and Blue Words: Depression and Gender in the Age of Self-Care* (New Brunswick, NJ: Rutgers University Press, 2010), 34–53.

4. Dana Crowley Jack, *Silencing the Self: Women and Depression* (Cambridge, MA: Harvard University Press, 1991), 29–36; Dana Crowley Jack and Alisha Ali, "Introduction: Culture, Self-Silencing, and Depression: A Contextual-Relational Perspective," in *Silencing the Self Across Cultures: Depression and Gender in the Social World*, ed. Dana Crowley Jack and Alisha Ali (Oxford: Oxford University Press, 2010), 3–18.

5. Tanja Zoellner and Susanne Hedlund, for example, conducted a study on German women that used Jack's "Silencing the Self Scale" to compare degrees of self-silencing in healthy women, depressed women, and agoraphobic women. Zoellner and Hedlund found that healthy women scored significantly lower on the "Silencing the Self Scale" ($M = 71.6$) than depressed women ($M = 100.6$), with agoraphobic women scoring in the middle ($M = 83.8$). Tanja Zoellner and Susanne Hedlund, "Women's Self-Silencing and Depression in the Socio-Cultural Context of Germany," in *Silencing the Self Across Cultures: Depression and Gender in the Social World*, ed. Dana Crowley Jack and Alisha Ali (Oxford: Oxford University Press, 2010), 128.

6. Maud Casey, "A Better Place to Live," in *Out of Her Mind: Women Writing on Madness*, ed. Rebecca Shannonhouse (New York: Modern Library, 2003), 178.

7. A 2002 report on women and depression published by the American Psychological Association, for example, mentions both the relatively high use of antidepressants by women and the link between depression and a common female "cognitive style" in

which a woman tends to "neglect the self in efforts to please and serve others" (called "unmitigated communion" in the report), but fails to address how this "cognitive style" might be an important factor in the high antidepressant use reported. Carolyn M. Mazure, Gwendolyn P. Keita, and Mary C. Blehar, *Summit on Women and Depression: Proceedings and Recommendations* (Washington, DC: American Psychological Association, 2002). One article that does address the connection is Richard Gordon's "Drugs Don't Talk," 47–72.

8. I am highlighting here a connection between two senses of the word "prescription": (1) a written direction for the preparation and use of medicine and (2) the action of giving an authoritative rule.

9. This observation follows in the footsteps of other authors who have analyzed how meaning is constructed in the context of depression. Recognizing the difficulty in light of the lived ambiguity of depression, Kimberly K. Emmons turns to the metaphors that people commonly use to make sense of depression. While Emmons primarily focuses on metaphors in speech, she turns her attention at one point to what medications come to symbolize for some patients. Emmons explains: "Manning and Solomon have been silenced by illness; the medications they ingest, however, seem to have gained a voice, or at least the ability to convey meaning. Solomon writes: 'Every morning and every night, I look at the pills in my hand: white, pink, red, turquoise. Sometimes they seem like writing in my hand, hieroglyphics saying that the future may be all right and that I owe it to myself to live and see.' Though the pills appear to be in an unknown and ancient language, they nevertheless convey hope, sanity, and a sense of future, which Solomon himself has lost." Emmons, *Black Dogs and Blue Words*, 120. This suggests that medication can acquire symbolic meaning, not just for a society, but for an individual person.

10. This suggestion is not meant to distract from other reasons why the vast majority of Americans diagnosed with depression and taking antidepressants today do not pursue any kind of psychotherapeutic treatment, even when recommended to do so by a physician. Insurance companies in the United States prefer cases to be handled as quickly and as cheaply as possible, and when compared to the prescription and management of antidepressant treatment by primary care physicians (see note 39 below), the costs and time required for psychotherapeutic treatment by a specialized therapist are almost always higher. Gordon, "Drugs Don't Talk," 65; Mazure, Keita, and Blehar, *Summit on Women and Depression*, 29.

11. Michel Foucault, *Madness and Civilization: A History of Insanity in the Age of Reason*, trans. Richard Howard (New York: Random House, 1965), x–xi.

12. Sigmund Freud, "Mourning and Melancholia," in *The Standard Edition of the Complete Psychological Works of Sigmund Freud* (London: Hogarth, 1975), 243.

13. In the *DSM-V*, symptoms like insomnia, decreased appetite, or diminished pleasure in activities are not indicators of depression unless they appear nearly every day for at least two weeks. This diagnostic criterion implies that such symptoms should not be taken as signs of mental illness if they occur in reaction to distress but do not linger beyond the two-week grace period. This means that, even when a clear trigger can be identified, one can only receive the diagnosis of depression if the trigger is present for longer than two weeks or if, after the trigger disappears, a person's response to it lingers on. American Psychiatric Association, *Diagnostic and Statistical Manual of Mental Disorders, Fifth Edition* (*DSM-V*) (Arlington, VA: American Psychiatric Publishing, 2013).

14. While women may be more likely to self-diagnose and self-report as depressed in many cultures, this two-to-one disparity is still strikingly consistent across cultures, suggesting that some aspect of women's experience regularly leads to depressive symptoms. On the transcultural character of this disparity, see Janet Stoppard, "Women's Bodies, Women's Lives and Depression: Toward a Reconciliation of Material and Discursive Accounts," in *Body Talk: The Material and Discursive Regulation of Sexuality, Madness, and Reproduction*, ed. Jane M. Ussher (New York: Routledge, 1997), 10–32; and

Jane Ussher, *Women's Madness: Misogyny or Mental Illness* (Amherst: University of Massachusetts Press, 1992).

15. Julia Kristeva, *Black Sun: Depression and Melancholia*, trans. Leon S. Roudiez (New York: Columbia University Press, 1989), 16.

16. John Lechte explains the importance of the transformation this way: "Language makes it possible for me to represent an object outside of myself; it enables me to symbolize a loss of my mother, that is, my separation from her. . . . For those who 'successfully' realize the separation, language arises to enable them to symbolize the sense of loss and suffering which ensues. Thus language, becoming more than a pure transparency, paradoxically brings each subject back to the mother once again, putting each individual in 'touch' with the world. This is to say that: I know words are only words, but at the same time I believe that these same words are a true link with objects—this is *denegation*." John Lechte, "Kristeva's *Soleil Noir* and Postmodernity," *Cultural Critique* 18, no. 18 (1991): 100.

17. Kristeva, *Black Sun*, 42.

18. I said earlier that a critical feminist standpoint requires that the self is relational and that we refrain from pathologizing deep social attachments the way that Freudian psychoanalysis might lead us to do. In light of this, I emphasize here that, even if one must overcome an infantile state of attachment in order to develop more complex interpersonal, linguistically mediated relationships, this does not require one to detach from the mother in the sense of withdrawing love and care.

19. Kristeva, *Black Sun*, 43.

20. Ibid., 23.

21. Ibid.

22. The work of Robin Lakoff has been particularly important for showing how the ways of speaking that women are typically habituated into are both formative and constraining for them. She examines the difference between language patterns typically used by men, patterns that tend to dominate in the public sphere, and language typically used by women, describing the psychological, social, and economic costs for women who must continually adapt from one to the other. "If she refuses to talk like a lady, she is ridiculed and subjected to criticism as unfeminine; if she does learn, she is ridiculed as unable to think clearly, unable to take part in a serious discussion: in some sense, as less than fully human. These two choices which a woman has—to be less than a woman or less than a person—are highly painful." Robin Lakoff, "Language and Women's Place," in *The Women and Language Debate: A Sourcebook*, ed. Camille Roman, Susan Juhasz, and Cristianne Miller (New Brunswick, NJ: Rutgers University Press, 1994), 282.

23. Kelly Oliver, *Subjectivity without Subjects: From Abject Fathers to Desiring Mothers* (Lanham, MD: Rowman & Littlefield, 1998), 52.

24. Jack and Ali, "Introduction: Culture, Self-Silencing, and Depression," 5.

25. Laura S. Brown, "Empowering Depressed Women: The Importance of a Feminist Lens," in *Silencing the Self Across Cultures: Depression and Gender in the Social World*, ed. Dana Crowley Jack and Alisha Ali (Oxford: Oxford University Press, 2010), 336.

26. David A. Karp, *Speaking of Sadness: Depression, Disconnection, and the Meanings of Illness* (Oxford: Oxford University Press, 1996), 36.

27. Jane M. Stoppard and Deanna J. Gammell, "Depressed Women's Treatment Experiences: Exploring Themes of Medicalization and Empowerment," in *Situating Sadness: Women and Depression in Social Context*, ed. Janet M. Stoppard and Linda M. McMullen (New York: New York University Press, 2003), 39–61; and Zoellner and Hedlund, "Women's Self-Silencing and Depression in the Socio-Cultural Context of Germany," 107–28.

28. Kristeva, *Black Sun*, 53.

29. Emil Kraepelin, "From 'Manic-Depressive Insanity' in Textbook Psychiatry, 8th edition, 1909–1915," in *The Nature of Melancholy: From Aristotle to Kristeva*, ed. Jennifer Radden (Oxford: Oxford University Press, 2000), 270.

30. Julia Kristeva and Dominique Grisoni, "Melancholia and Creation: An Interview with Dominique Grisoni," in *Julia Kristeva Interviews*, ed. Ross Mitchell Guberman (New York: Columbia University Press, 1996), 80.

31. Ibid.

32. Julia Kristeva, *Intimate Revolt: The Powers and Limits of Psychoanalysis*, trans. Jeanine Herman (New York: Columbia University Press, 2002), 20.

33. Kristeva, *Black Sun*, 55.

34. Ibid., 56.

35. Ibid.

36. The intensity of an affective dimension of depression is clear in Maud Casey's account, as is her yearning to cling once again to the mother's body: "During the weeks my mother spent in Illinois, my sister would sleep over on occasional nights. In her white nightgown with lace fringe around the neck, she was a radiant beauty. . . . She was my fairy-tale princess and my tentacles slithered out of their alien pod, wrapping themselves around her. . . . 'I want to go back to the hospital,' I would whisper to my mother trying to sleep next to me. 'I want to die.' 'I want to go home,' I would say to my sister as she rolled over to hold my shaking hands. The three—hospital, death, home—became interchangeable. 'Tell me what's going on,' my mother would whisper back, her warm body charged and ready like a nightlight, glowing with the possibility of emergency." Casey, "A Better Place to Live," 178.

37. Julia Kristeva, *This Incredible Need to Believe*, trans. Beverly Bie Brahic (New York: Columbia University Press, 2009), 81.

38. Kristeva, *Black Sun*, 24.

39. Sara Beardsworth, *Julia Kristeva: Psychoanalysis and Modernity* (Albany: State University of New York Press, 2004), 109.

40. Several events over the past fifty years have led to the rise of medicalized psychiatry including, notably, the Health Management Organization (HMO) Act of 1973, which triggered the explosive growth of quick, low-cost pharmaceutical treatments offered by general practitioners with no expertise in mental health. For a helpful discussion of this history, see Kevin Aho and Charles Guignon, "Medicalized Psychiatry and the Talking Cure: A Hermeneutic Intervention," *Human Studies* 34, no. 3 (2011): 293–308.

41. See J. L. Austin, *How To Do Things with Words* (Cambridge, MA: Harvard University Press, 1975), 99–100.

42. Jacques Lacan, "The Direction of Treatment and the Principles of Its Power," in *Écrits*, trans. Bruce Fink (New York: W. W. Norton, 2006), 520.

43. Kristeva, *Intimate Revolt*, 23.

SIX

Language as Habitat

Doing Justice to Experiences of Linguistic Alienation

Language, we have seen, plays an essential role in our lives. It is language through which we develop understanding and direction, and it is through language that we come to terms with experience. My aim in the previous three chapters has been to illustrate some of the ways that Continental philosophers have arrived at this realization about language by looking closely at what happens when a person's relationship to language becomes troubled—when, for example, going through trauma or losing oneself in a pattern of self-silencing. In such cases, we have seen that recovery requires finding one's voice and regaining the desire and confidence to collaborate with others in the activity of world disclosure. It requires that a person's way of inhabiting the world as a linguistic being, so precarious in its initial development, be built back up again. For Continental philosophers, then, sensitivity to how the linguistic mode of being can collapse or otherwise fall into disrepair reveals the precarity of language's power as a mode of world disclosure. This precarity comes to light, however, not only when we recognize the existence of such frustrations, but also from the fact that we regularly experience joy and fulfillment in the activity of speech. We can feel joy when we manage to articulate or communicate something difficult or when we feel we have understood another where we feared we might not. Taken together, these experiences of linguistic fulfillment and frustration reveal how the linguistic being is not a static property of human beings but an active way of *being* in the world.

We've seen in previous chapters, then, the careful attention that Continental philosophers have given to this internal dynamic of our linguistic being. Initially, we considered Continental theories that presented the development of language as the fulfillment of the human need for meaning and direction. In subsequent chapters, the focus shifted to the frustrations humans experience in seeking such fulfillment. Here we considered, for example, the way that Continental philosophers read the literature of the Holocaust as the effort of survivors to communicate and come to terms with trauma and the loss of meaning. And in the previous two chapters we explored the profound forms of alienation that can occur when a person comes to identify so much in the role of the listener that she struggles to act as a participant in the interpretation of her own life's meaning. These, then, are some of the ways that the disclosive power of language can ebb and flow throughout a person's life.

Such dynamics are important to contemporary research on the harm people suffer under epistemic injustice.[1] Still, they have not traditionally been regarded as important to philosophy of language. This is nowhere clearer than in the case of linguistic determinism, according to which each language by itself determines the way that the world is disclosed to its speakers.[2] In this view, language is a force that so influences our thinking that its reliability and epistemic authority in our lives is always guaranteed. Individual speakers can thus neither suffer alienation from nor experience joy in the language they speak. Instead, one is guaranteed that the world is always disclosed in the same way. As a speaker of a given language, that language is one's "epistemic worldview."

The appeal of this claim is broad. In chapter 4, we considered its popularization alongside the rise of identity politics. Its appeal is also evident, though, in the work of several influential thinkers over the past century who have in some way been associated with the "linguistic turn" in philosophy, arguably one of the strongest common threads linking disparate philosophical traditions over the past century. Within the early analytic tradition, Ludwig Wittgenstein, for example, famously argued that the limits of one's language are the limits of one's world.[3] The pragmatist philosopher, Richard Rorty, makes a similar case, arguing that the debt of thinking to language requires philosophers to abandon the search for foundational truths beyond a given vocabulary. This is an epistemological argument. For Rorty, "we have no prelinguistic consciousness to which language needs to be adequate, no deep sense of how things are which it is the duty of philosophers to spell out in language. . . . What is described as our consciousness is simply a disposition to use the language of our ancestors, to worship the corpses of their metaphors."[4]

Despite the popularization of the theory of linguistic determinism and its continuation in the philosophy of the linguistic turn, the theory has raised serious concerns for some. Philosophy's fundamental purpose, after all, is to promote critical reflection on the beliefs and habits of thinking that one has taken for granted—something that I have tried to demonstrate in the previous two chapters with the help of Continental feminist philosophy. For the linguistic determinist, though, there is no possibility of critiquing or transforming one's epistemic worldview. It is entrenched irremediably into the language that we speak. Thus it would seem that, if philosophy embraces linguistic determinism, it must abandon its most cherished aspirations—critical thinking and the pursuit of knowledge.

Continental philosophers in particular have been accused of promoting this dangerous theory of language. This is particularly the case with so-called postmodern philosophers like Judith Butler and Jacques Derrida. Commentators Gerald Graff and David Novitz find in statements like the infamous one from Derrida's *Of Grammatology* that there is "nothing outside of the text" evidence of a linguistic determinism that is ultimately detrimental to the project of philosophy.[5] For Graff and Novitz, Derrida is arguing that the reality we know is nothing but the impress of language, one that a speaker of that language cannot critique. It is not only the "postmodern" philosophers who have been accused of linguistic determinism, however. The same reading has been offered of Martin Heidegger's phenomenological account of the role of language in setting forth a world. It was, after all, Heidegger's attentiveness to how our present ways of thinking are greatly indebted to the historical language of metaphysics that most influenced Derrida's project of deconstruction. For this reason, Cristina Lafont situates Heidegger in what she identifies as the linguistic turn in German hermeneutical philosophy. For Heidegger, according to Lafont, language continues to be a historical inheritance that ultimately renders tragically inadequate our knowledge of the world as well as our ability to communicate with others.[6] Likewise, Jürgen Habermas argues that, for Heidegger, the language of being is something "absolutely unmediated," "a contingent occurrence to which Dasein is delivered over" and to whose authority Dasein must ultimately bow.[7]

What such readings miss, however, is precisely the precarity and the dynamic ebb and flow of linguistic identification. These authors see neither the sense of fulfillment that takes place with linguistic identification nor the sense of alienation that occurs with its diminishment. In turn, they overlook an essential feature of worldhood itself, namely, its reiterative character. In this final chapter, then, I want to highlight some of the sources within Continental philosophy of language that challenge the model of linguistic determinism it has often been associated with and also bring to light what is so important about its challenge to this theory. I begin by returning to Martin Heidegger's work on language, introduced in the first two chapters, to show how a theory that takes language as our primary mode of world disclosure needn't take language as a deterministic force. In the first half of the chapter, I develop these points by applying Heidegger's analysis of "unreadiness-to-hand" in *Being and Time* to the topic of language use, explaining how the analysis reveals the reiterative character of ready-to-hand language and thus accounts for the possibility of speakers who develop a reflexive, critical relationship to the very language in which they are immersed. From here, I go on to explain how this analysis has proven to be a useful resource for Continental political thought. While Heidegger himself does not draw out the implications of his analysis for a study of power, I show that Derrida does just this in *Monolingualism of the Other*, where he describes the reflexive, critical relationship he has to the French language, his own mother tongue, and uses this as an opportunity to reflect on the nature of political power. Over and against the linguistic determinist, then, for whom language is an epistemic worldview immune to philosophical critique, I argue that, for Heidegger and Derrida, linguistic worldhood is always the result of a reiterative process—the ongoing task of world disclosure but also at times, as Derrida argues, a process of "politico-phantasmatic construction."[8]

HEIDEGGER ON LANGUAGE AND TRADITION

It is, on the one hand, not surprising for readers to associate Heidegger's account of the relationship between language and world with linguistic determinism. After all, it is Heidegger's aim in *Being and Time* to show that, in its most basic form, the world that appears to us is not the result of cognition produced in the encounter between subject and object but is set forth through our practical dealings, a world in which we as reflective subjects find ourselves always already entangled. Language is part of this setting forth. For the most part, we use language without thinking about it. We take the words, phrases, and rhetorical forms that we hear—language that we have acquired over time—to disclose the world immediately. This is what Heidegger means when he says that the primordial meaning of *logos* is *apophasis*—"letting an entity be seen from itself," adding that "this pointing-out has in view the entity itself and not, let us say, a mere 'representation' [*Vorstellung*] of it."[9] Lawrence Hatab gives the following example to illustrate this point. He points out that when we hear the phrase "your child has been in an accident," we do not first pause and ponder what this could mean, but respond according to what has immediately been disclosed through the statement—the danger the child is in.[10] In the practical dealings of everyday life, propositions tend to function as immediately disclosive for us in this way.

As we saw in the first chapter, this account of language follows from the exposition Heidegger gives in *Being and Time* of Dasein's being-in-the-world. Recall that Dasein's being-in-the-world refers simply to the way that we first encounter beings and the way that, for the most part, we continue to encounter them. Our mode of being, Heidegger claims, is to be in the midst of beings. This means that "proximally and for the most part," as Heidegger says, we do not encounter things as objects of reflection or detached theoretical contemplation. They appear to us in the flow of our practical activities. Yet we tend not to recognize this about our-selves. We become absorbed in what we let be seen, such that we become oblivious to the processes that provide this illumination. For Heidegger, the activity of speech constitutes an important mode of our being-in-the-world, but we rarely reflect on the language we rely upon constantly to set forth the world. We use it without giving it much thought and take for granted that it is perfectly suited for the practical ends that it has enabled. We take it to naturally fit the world, rarely reflecting on the history of this fitness or what other possibilities of understanding might be foreclosed by the illumination it provides.

Given Heidegger's emphasis on our immersion in the world and our tendency to blind ourselves to this immersion, it seems quite tempting to read Heidegger as presenting language as an epistemic worldview that we cannot step outside of, even as philosophers interested in truth. Thus, it may seem that Heidegger's argument supports the theory of linguistic determinism, presenting language as a force that constructs the world we live in and unequivocally constrains thinking. Indeed, Rorty reads Heidegger's writing as bringing us face-to-face with the historical and cultural contingency of the metaphysical language we rely on, "reminding us," as Rorty says, "that this language is not that of 'human reason' but is the creation of the thinkers of our historical past."[11] The determining force of such inheritance is, for Rorty, far reaching. Citing Heidegger's *On the Way to Language*, Rorty explains, "For there will be no way to rise above the language, culture, institutions, and practices one has adopted and view all these on par with all the others. . . . Or, to put the point in Heidegger's way, 'language speaks man.'"[12]

Taken alone, it is not hard to see how one derives such an interpretation of Heidegger from a declaration like "language speaks man," but is Rorty right to assume that, for Heidegger, finding oneself in a linguistic tradition involves finding one's thinking thoroughly conditioned by a vocabulary that it cannot "rise above," that is, that it can neither affirm nor critique? Is it right to say that, for Heidegger, language simply *determines* Dasein's world as an epistemic worldview—a simple, sovereign presence in the face of which reflection is powerless? Or is there already in the work of Heidegger, a seminal figure within Continental philosophy of language, a reckoning with the oscillation of linguistic identification and the place of critical reflection in linguistic being?

First, let us notice that Rorty's interpretation misses the force of Heidegger's refrain: "proximally and for the most part" [*zunächst und zumeist*]. Heidegger uses this refrain throughout *Being and Time* to mark the fact that Dasein's everyday, habitual way of being-in-the-world where it is oblivious to its own world-disclosive activity is not the only kind of comportment possible. To say that another comportment is possible is not to say that Dasein can shed its character of being-in-the-world. If we could do this, we would cease to be Dasein. We can, however, become more reflective and aware of our mode of existence.

This possibility becomes clear if we consider Heidegger's description of his task in *Being and Time* as the "destruction" [*Destruktion*] of precisely those formulations of being that are most deeply ingrained in our tradition.[13] By destruction, Heidegger does not intend a rejection of the formulations that we have come to rely on to disclose the world and, with this, "a vicious relativizing of ontological standpoints."[14] The point is, rather, to open a space for reflection on these traditional formulations so that we inherit them in a more thoughtful way. Heidegger describes the task as follows:

> Tradition takes what has come down to us and delivers it over to self-evidence; it blocks our access to those primordial "sources" from which the categories and concepts handed down to us have been in part quite genuinely drawn. Indeed it makes us forget that they have had such an origin, and makes us suppose that the necessity of going back to these sources is something which we need not even understand. . . . If the question of Being is to have its own history made transparent then this hardened tradition must be loosened up, and the concealments which it has brought about must be dissolved.[15]

While Heidegger recognizes, then, the way concepts passed down through tradition come to appear to us as self-evident, he also sees that it is possible to reflect on these concepts, removing from them and the world they set forth their aura of self-evidence.[16] Now, in his remarks on destruction, Heidegger is speaking specifically about the destruction of traditional formulations of the question of being, but the point applies to language more broadly—not least of all because language plays such an important role in preserving the legacies of traditional ontology. For the most part, we treat linguistic formulations that we habitually use to interpret the world as the only ones possible, and we neglect to consider the historical character of these interpretations. We can, however, become more reflective. We can develop a better appreciation for the perennial problems within which these concepts once arose, and, in so doing, we can better assess their value for our purposes today. We can, in other words, engage in critical reflection.

It is not only Heidegger but twentieth-century Continental philosophy in general that tends to encourage this critical reflection on discourse. This is clear, for example, in the way that several strands of Continental feminist philosophy treat historical discourse. Recall, for instance, my discussion of Butler's genealogy of the category of sex in chapter 4. I argued that Butler's exposition of the profound impact of the historical discourse of sex on our lives is precisely what allows her to come to recognize other possibilities for gendered existence. Likewise, in chapter 5, we saw how Julia Kristeva takes the medical discourse of diagnosis—

and in particular the diagnosis of depression—and attempts to think anew about the fundamental problem in response to which this discourse arose. By considering the perennial problem of women's subordination, Kristeva is able to interrogate the medical discourse of depression and, in so doing, to bring the broader phenomenon of depression to light so as to better understand the role of silence in it. Such an analysis, I have argued, then enables us to better understand the constraints of this particular discourse, to think more clearly about when it is and is not useful, and to imagine other possible responses to the problem of depression. Heidegger himself subjects the discourse of psychiatry to such critical reflection in his *Zollikon Seminars*, explaining that it is his primary intention to encourage the physicians in attendance to reflect more on the history of the scientific discourse they habitually rely on in their work as psychiatrists.[17]

As historical beings, the traditions that we inherit can always become objects of reflection for us. Sometimes, however, critical reflection is precipitated by an event that suddenly disrupts our usual obliviousness toward the process of world disclosure. In *Being and Time*, Heidegger describes this kind of disruption as a modification of the ready-to-hand, what he calls "unreadiness-to-hand" [*Unzuhandenheit*]. Normally, the process of world disclosure happens without our reflecting on the process; however, our attitude changes when we discover something conspicuously unusable, missing, or in the way, that is, when we discover something unready-to-hand. Heidegger's famous illustration of this in *Being and Time* is the malfunctioning of a hammer. When immersed in the flow of hammering a nail, we focus on the end we are striving to achieve and not on each element and incremental step in the process that allows us to achieve this end. If, however, the hammer breaks in the midst of hammering, then, Heidegger says, we not only notice the unusable hammer, but "the context of equipment is lit up, not as something never seen before, but as a totality constantly sighted beforehand in circumspection."[18] Similarly, when I am healthy and able-bodied, I pay no mind to all the bodily elements and processes that work together in intricate harmony to allow me to inhabit the world as I usually do. But when I become ill or sustain a serious injury, I suddenly see the important work that all of these parts and functions perform and the contingency of the world that, when functioning normally, they enable. This is why Heidegger says that, during such disruptions, "the world announces itself."[19]

In his discussion of unreadiness-to-hand in *Being and Time*, Heidegger unfortunately does not discuss the possibility of encountering conspicuous, obstinate, or obtrusive speech. However, it is not hard to see that the sudden disruption in the reliability of everyday language, the language we use typically without reflecting on this activity, accomplishes a similar illumination. This is, after all, clear from what we have explored in previous chapters. In chapter 3, for example, we saw how the disruption in linguistic being experienced by survivors of trauma brought to light for Continental philosophers like Derrida the precarity of this mode of being. Similarly, in chapter 5, our exploration of the withdrawal from language that accompanies depression brought to light, as in chapter 3, the vital role played by others in sustaining one's linguistic identification. Heidegger does not address situations like these in *Being and Time*; however, the analysis of unreadiness-to-hand that he offers there can easily be applied in such cases to help account for why some philosophers have taken such situations to be so instructive. They provide the perfect opportunity to reflect on the important role that language plays in our lives.

Although Heidegger does not directly discuss such disruptions in language in *Being and Time*, he later makes this connection in his lectures on "The Nature of Language," discussed earlier in chapter 2. Recall that Heidegger's aim in these lectures is to bring us to a point where we can undergo an experience of language. This is important, he explains, because it will bring about a transformation in our mode of existence.

> To undergo an experience [*Erfahrung*] with language, then, means to let ourselves be properly concerned by the claim of language by entering into and submitting to it. If it is true that man finds the proper abode of his existence in language—whether he is aware of it or not—then an experience we undergo with language will touch the innermost nexus of our existence. We who speak language may thereupon become transformed by such experiences, from one day to the next or in the course of time.[20]

Heidegger goes on to explain that, for the most part, we do not undergo an experience with language. We speak it. In the midst of this speaking, however, "our relation to language is vague, obscure, even speechless."[21] This happens necessarily as we use speech to accomplish our practical dealings. Still, it is possible to undergo an experience of language and thereby change one's relationship to it. This can happen, Heidegger explains, precisely "when we cannot find the right word for something that concerns us, carries us away, oppresses or encourages us"[22]—in other words, when the flow of our usual linguistic activity is disrupted.

Heidegger does not mention the concept of unreadiness-to-hand from *Being and Time* here; however, it is not hard to see that this experience of language as suddenly obtrusive or missing is illuminating in the same way the breakdown of the hammer or an injury to the body is. It brings to light what typically withdraws into the background of our lives. That is, it illuminates the intricate web of mediating processes that we typically ignore as we go about our practical activities, absorbed in the world that they quietly set forth.

But such disruptions reveal something else as well. They reveal a point, within the process of world disclosure, where that process appears quite contingent. They reveal, in other words, a moment of instability in it. Because any world rests upon the reiteration of world disclosure, the existence of this background environment is never guaranteed. Reiteration is essential. This is what we forget when we become absorbed in a system of language that discloses the world in a certain way, and it is what we can be made to recall quite forcefully when we undergo a serious disruption in the reliability of our linguistic world.

Heidegger addresses this point about instability in his discussion of idle talk in *Being and Time*, examined in chapter 1. This, recall, is where Heidegger considers how public discourse can provide an illusory ground for thinking—how we can become absorbed in customary ways of speaking such that we forget what makes this customariness possible and, in turn, blind ourselves to other possibilities. To forget this is, in Heidegger's terms, to inhabit language in an "inauthentic" [*uneigentlich*] way, taking everything as "genuinely understood, genuinely taken hold of, genuinely spoken," even when it is not.[23] It is inauthentic not because it involves inheriting a language that we did not author ourselves, as then authenticity would be equivalent to worldlessness, but because it overlooks the process by which the ready-to-hand is sustained and thus the inherent instability in the world of meaning into which we are, for the most part, absorbed.

This instability is, however, denied by linguistic determinists. A linguistic determinist's thinking remains beholden to some inaugural event of language that happened in the past—an inheritance that bestows that person with an epistemic worldview, which shall remain fixed for as long as that language system is in place. This is, of course, one way of understanding the legacy of metaphysical language, namely, as the residue of past intellectual events into which we were once fatefully thrown. In understanding the power of language this way, however, what remains unaccounted for is how a worldview, or even the linguistic system that gives rise to it, is reiterated over time. Any historicist account would necessarily overlook this question, since it presumes that history is the power of the past to unilaterally influence the present and that such a power exists independent of any conditions.

In *Being and Time*, however, Heidegger is clear that Dasein's facticity is not like the *factum brutum* of something present-at-hand. As he explains, for Dasein, "The that-it-is of facticity never becomes something that we can come across by beholding it," and thus, "Thrownness is neither a fact that is finished nor a fact that is settled. Dasein's facticity is such that as long as it is what it is, Dasein remains in the throw."[24] For Heidegger, it is not just that each of us is cast into a history of language once and for all—one that we have no choice but to content ourselves with from that point on, given the intractable direction of time's flow. Understood this way, such a condition of being thrown, not to mention of being historical, would be a condition external to Dasein's being. It would be something

Dasein passively endures, something that happens to befall it. Such a characterization, though, misses how thrownness is intrinsic to Dasein's being.

We can now see clearly how Heidegger's philosophy of language challenges rather than supports this popular view of language as a unilaterally determining force. To see language as deterministic is to fashion it as a sovereign presence, one whose claim on us requires no effort of preservation but is simply guaranteed. In this view, there is no need for a repetition of world disclosure at work in language because, by the linear movement of history, its having once taken place keeps it perpetually in motion. But for Heidegger, the language that we inherit, like any part of tradition, is never simply behind us. Although we tend to treat it as something settled in this way, it is always possible to relate to this inheritance differently. What we cannot do is to simply rid ourselves of the way that historical language sets forth the world for us. We can, however, learn to *dwell* with this inheritance differently—giving proper attention to both the world-disclosive power of language and the contingencies that are inherent to it. It is precisely this task of dwelling—or, to use Heidegger's earlier term, this task of *Destruktion*—that later Continental philosophers engaged in a productive critical reflection on historical language make central to their own philosophical work. We turn now to one place in the recent Continental tradition where this influence is quite evident, namely, Derrida's *Monolingualism of the Other; or, the Prosthesis of Origin*.

DERRIDA ON COLONIALITY AS LINGUISTIC ALIENATION

Derrida gave the lecture he would later publish as *Monolingualism of the Other* at Louisiana State University in 1992 at a conference on the topic of *francophonie* outside France titled "Echoes from Elsewhere"/"*Renvois d'ailleurs*." At the beginning of the lecture, Derrida invites us to imagine a "subject of French culture" coming to us and telling us "in good French": "I only have one language, yet it is not mine."[25] Or, as he elaborates:

> I am monolingual. My monolingualism dwells, and I call it my dwelling; it feels like one to me, and I remain in it and inhabit it. It inhabits me. The monolingualism in which I draw my very breath is, for me, my element. Not a natural element, not the transparency of the ether, but an absolute habitat [*un milieu absolu*]. . . . It constitutes me, it dictates even the ipseity of all things to me, and also prescribes a monastic solitude for me; as if, even before learning to speak, I had been bound by some vows.[26]

As the lecture goes on, we come to understand that this subject of French culture is Derrida himself—or Derrida as he thinks through his own relationship to the French language as an Algerian Jew who grew up speaking French and who for most of his life had French citizenship. This is reflected in Derrida's description of his relationship to the French language. By his own admission, he has a strong identification with the French language. It is his mother tongue. As such, it is the language that dictates to him "even the ipseity of all things," that is, that grants him an epistemic worldview. It operates for him, to use Heidegger's language, as a ready-to-hand means of disclosure—constituting a world for him that is set forth independent of any reflection. This is what Derrida means when he identifies as "monolingual." Yet Derrida tells us that, at the same time, this language that he has inherited in such a thorough way is not simply ready-to-hand. It lacks the transparency of a "natural element." It is instead a habitat [*milieu*] and a way of dwelling [*demeure*]. But what could this mean, and why would Derrida want to insist on such a description?

Derrida points out that his description will immediately solicit criticism from philosophers who will accuse him of performative contradiction and even of insincerity. Since the description itself relies on the French language as a means of expression, some philosophers will claim that the deed of the statement itself proves the opposite of what is asserted. Spoken in perfectly good French, they will say, the statement shows that French is no foreign language to the speaker. It is perfectly reliable and familiar. It has the perfect transparency of a worldview that one can never transcend or step outside of. "You do not believe what you are saying," they will protest, and "you want to mislead us. And now in order to stir us and win us to your cause, there you are, playing the card of the exile and immigrant worker, there you are, claiming, in French, that French has always been a foreign language to you!"[27]

In truth, Derrida's description of his relationship to the French language might easily solicit such objections from those familiar with the history of his native Algeria. Of all the predominantly Arab countries colonized by the French, Algeria was, by most accounts, the most thoroughly transformed by French culture. Until the revolution in 1962, French had been adopted into almost every corner of Algerian culture—not only government but education, religion, and eventually nearly all aspects of cultural life.[28] Like most Algerians of his day, French was the language that Derrida spoke at home and in which he was educated. Thus, very early on, Derrida's world was bound up with the French language and culture, so much so that it would not have dawned on him at the time to identify as an Algerian Jew assimilated into French culture or to think about the history of *francophonie* throughout the Maghreb.

Had Derrida identified strongly with Jewish culture as a child, this might have been different. However, like most other Maghrebi Jews at the time, living in a predominantly Muslim land that had been colonized by a predominantly Christian state for more than a century, Derrida did not identify strongly with Judaism. As he notes, nothing comparable to the Yiddish language was available to him growing up, whereas elsewhere this served to preserve Jewish identity for others in the diaspora.

Moreover, as an effect of French colonial power, many Jewish rituals had been given Christian names and were inflected with Christian significance.

Understandably, then, Derrida explains that he found his intellectual identity as a young student within the rich landscape of French literature, the one part of his education that he reports having enjoyed. This eventually led him to continue his education and his philosophical career in France—an undertaking that would only further consolidate his linguistic identification with the French language. Not only in the early years of his life, then, but also increasingly over the period of his intellectual development, Derrida invested in the French language as his fundamental mode of world disclosure and, along the way, sought to rid himself of any trace of his Algerian French accent. Yet, again, Derrida insists that this same language from which he claims to draw his breath is, despite all of this, not a "natural element" for him but only a "habitat," a "way of dwelling." Is it the case, then, that Derrida's statement really is dishonest? If not, what could possibly account for this?

Part of Derrida's description of his relationship to the French language can be explained by considering how residents of colonized lands generally strive to adopt the cultural and linguistic style of the colonial government, and how colonialism tends to produce in colonized people what Rey Chow calls "an unfulfillable yearning for linguistic purity." [29] On top of this, Derrida's relationship to the French language must also be explained by considering the history of political events affecting the fate of Algerian Jews in particular. Because of their Jewish ethnicity, Derrida's family members were not citizens but subjects of France, with limited rights until the *Crémieux Decree* of 1870. Even after the decree, though, Derrida explains that the status of his own French identity often felt precarious. This was particularly the case during the Vichy period, when Derrida was a boy, and Algerian Jews were stripped of their French citizenship. Derrida was forbidden to attend school for a year based on his Jewish ethnicity. It is no wonder, then, that Derrida describes his relationship to the French language as he does. In such a case, most people would readily make an exception to the normal rule of linguistic and cultural determinism. Indeed, they might even support a political initiative to reissue parts of Algerian culture as they existed before colonization.

But according to Derrida, his relationship to language is not exceptional. It is "exemplary of a universal structure" and "represents or reflects a type of originary 'alienation' [*aliénation*] that institutes every language as a language of the other [*toute langue en langue de l'autre*]." [30] If one were to miss this part of the argument and take Derrida to be presenting his story as exceptional, his story could then be seen to confirm the way that the linguistic determinist understands language, worldview, and identity. We would see someone caught between cultures and presume this is the reason for not feeling completely determined by a language. It would confirm for us that language can only ever feel alien when one doesn't have a single language transmitted through a single culture.[31] Only then, we expect, should one feel caught between worlds. The presumption then is that one's "own" language, that familiar habitat, can never by itself be strange to the one who inherits it and lags behind it.

Derrida's positing of an originary alienation that makes every language a language of the other has been controversial. Geoffrey Bennington, for example, argues that Derrida's claim seems to problematically conflate the situation of different political subjects (e.g., treating as synonymous the Kosovar Albanian, the Tibetan exile, and the English-speaking native-born American in Dallas), and, moreover, to justify or at least present as inevitable "the very coloniality that the point is to protest against."[32] In Bennington's reading, the text seems to both assert the inevitability of this originary alienation and to protest against it on normative political-ethical grounds. If we read Derrida's remark in the context of Heidegger's exploration of language as I have developed here, however, we can appreciate how Derrida's point allows for an important distinction between the otherness of two forms of language. Indeed, as we will see, this distinction will prove pivotal for the protest against coloniality that Bennington rightly sees being staged in Derrida's lecture.

There is a sense then, on the one hand, that every language is the language of the other and thus represents, as Derrida says, a kind of originary alienation. This is because of the basic condition in which all human beings, as historical, come to acquire a language. As Heidegger explains, we find ourselves in a world that has always already been understood and interpreted and that remains sustained—albeit precariously—by a set of reiterative processes that are mostly inconspicuous. Although it is possible to become reflective about our inheritance of specific discourse traditions, we tend to take these traditions for granted. Their history therefore tends to remain shrouded in obscurity. As we saw earlier, this point becomes central to the social and ethical philosophy of feminist philosopher Judith Butler, who emphasizes the *unchosen* character of the linguistic being's thrownness into discourse. It is also, however, central to Derrida, who recognizes the general difficulties faced when embarking on an autobiographical recollection of one's relationship to language. Since that language is acting as one's mode of disclosure, it is impossible to completely bracket out its effect. Or, as Derrida puts it, the "I" that would embark on that pursuit would have formed itself "at the site of a *situation* that cannot be found, a site always referring elsewhere, to something other, to another language, to the other in general."[33] This is, then, one form of language's otherness.

According to Heidegger, though, as we have just seen, it is a mistake to understand Dasein's historicity as a one-sided determination of the present by the past. This point is significant for Heidegger: if we are to develop a more authentic relationship to the traditions we inherit, then we must come to see how we actively preserve in the present certain interpretations of the past precisely by taking these interpretations for granted. Similarly, Derrida argues that if we were to then posit this event of language as the simple *factum brutum* of an origin, we would then fail to acknowledge the way that inheritance of language is continually renewed and transformed in the present. In a later interview on the *Monolingualism* lecture, Derrida describes this in terms of a necessary counter-signing that takes place whenever one inherits or receives a language. Derrida explains:

> When one is born into a language, one inherits it because it is there before us, it is older than us, its law precedes us. One starts by recognizing its law, that is to say, its law, grammar, all this being almost ageless. But to inherit is not simply to receive passively something that is already there, like a possession. To inherit is to reaffirm through transformation, change, and displacement. . . . An inheritance must be signed; it must be counter-signed—that is to say, at bottom, one must leave one's signature on inheritance itself, on the language one receives. That is a contradiction: one receives and, at the same time, one gives.[34]

It is because the inheritance of a language inevitably involves "transformation, change, and displacement" that the French language appears to Derrida as a system whose meaning is not guaranteed in advance but rests precariously on a "way of dwelling" in relation to the past. It is inherited by the present, not "passively" as a "possession" to be passed down, but as a mode of world disclosure that is always underway, always mediated by the contemporary age.[35] However, as with Heidegger, this is once again not to deny the facticity of linguistic inheritance or the interpretive traditions that it sets forth for us, but to consider the mediating conditions that preserve any such inheritance. It is in light of this ongoing task of inheriting the discursive traditions of the past, then, that Derrida claims that language is always an "other," that his relationship to language is not exceptional but "exemplary of a universal structure."

But Derrida's desire to highlight this point of instability also has another motive, namely, to expose the political manipulations that deny it and so configure language as a "natural element." Just as Heidegger recognized the human tendency to deny the limits of the readiness-to-hand into which we are absorbed, Derrida recognizes the use of such a denial in the construction and preservation of hegemonic power. Such denial leads to concrete forms of alienation and hegemony. And so, while there is no overcoming the first sense of language's otherness described above—that "originary 'alienation' that institutes every language as a language of the other," Derrida indeed protests against this modified form of alienation. This, then, is the target of Derrida's normative political-ethical argument—not language's otherness as such. As he writes:

> Because the master does not possess exclusively, and naturally, what
> he calls his language, because, whatever he wants or does, he cannot
> maintain any relations of property or identity that are natural, national,
> congenital, or ontological, with it, because he can give substance to and
> articulate [*dire*] this appropriation only in the course of an unnatural
> process of politico-phantasmatic constructions, because language is not
> his natural possession, he can, thanks to that very fact, pretend histori-
> cally, through the rape of a cultural usurpation, which means always
> essentially colonial, to appropriate it in order to impose it as "his own."
> That is his belief; he wishes to make others share it through the use of
> force or cunning [*par la force ou par la ruse*]; he wants to make others
> believe it, as they do a miracle, through rhetoric, the school, or the
> army. It suffices for him, through whatever means there is, to make
> himself understood, to have his "speech act" work, to create conditions
> for that.[36]

Here Derrida analyzes a dimension of language's power of world disclosure that Heidegger does not, namely, the way that this power can be sustained by the political manipulation of social arrangements. In such cases, language's power as a mode of world disclosure becomes supported by "an unnatural process of politico-phantasmatic constructions" which through "force and cunning" ensures the felicity of certain speech acts. In turn, it serves to reinforce the might of such constructions—transforming them from force to power.[37]

We can understand this point clearly if we consider the capacity to name and its relationship to power. Naming requires an intricate social convention—not just the will of one linguistic being to bestow a name. Without others to accept one's naming ritual, nobody could exercise their capacity to give new names. But as we saw in the previous chapter on the power of medical diagnosis, in a society where there is an unequal distribution of hermeneutic authority, this capacity to give names is made to appear as the exclusive possession of a limited number of actors and institutions who exercise this capacity in a way that renders this power invisible to all those who are denied it. In a society structured in this way, the ability to name and rename is made to appear as a natural, inevitable right of such actors rather than an expression of power. Thus, it is not hard to see why the colonial forces of France insisted upon translating Jewish rituals into the idiom of Christianity or, for that matter, on renaming Algerian cities and streets with names that commemorate French history and that celebrate ancient Romans "as the imperial progenitors of the French in Africa."[38] It is, in part, through such acts of naming and renaming that colonial force is consolidated into colonial power. The history of such a transformation becomes largely forgotten while the world of meaning that is set forth remains in place.

Essential to political power, then, is the naturalizing of certain ways of speaking—of disclosing the world—and the delegitimizing of other ways. In this situation, those disempowered by the power structure will find themselves discouraged from reflecting on this history and will find their critique of colonial power foreclosed in advance by the forces of naturalization that consolidate this power. For them, language will often feel alienating, because they are discouraged from cultivating a critical, historical relationship to their language. This, then, is the second sense in which language can become alien to a person. And it is the system of hegemonic political power that produces this specific kind of alienation that is the subject of Derrida's normative political-ethical critique.

And yet, if we look critically at this system of hegemonic political power, we can come to see that the conditions that satisfy the efficacy of a ritual are never as settled as they appear. We can reflect on the history of *francophonie*, for example. This was the subject of the conference at which Derrida gave this lecture, after all. Moreover, as part of a language that is always underway, any given discourse remains open to contestation. There is always room for debate about whether a speech-act works. France's redesignation of Jewish rituals, for example, could have been contested, the infelicity of the names challenged even after they were commonly accepted. Or, like the Algerians did after the revolution, the names of cities and streets could have been changed to better reflect the Arab and Muslim history of Algeria that French colonial forces sought to leave behind. When such things are done without the authority of a political regime, they are, of course, risky.[39] One risks being misunderstood and criticized by those who benefit from the political arrangement that has been naturalized by the traditional discourse now being revised. In the face of such risks, many simply resign themselves to the current arrangement, remaining alienated within its discourse.

Derrida's protest against the conditions that give rise to this kind of alienation marks a point of difference from Heidegger's otherwise quite parallel account that I have sketched above. While Heidegger insists that inauthenticity does not entail any moral failure, Derrida intends precisely to expose the ethical and political shortcomings of those who manipulate social arrangements so that certain forms of language can remain unproblematically ready-to-hand while access to their history, along with other possible ways of speaking, is foreclosed. It is to such people that Derrida speaks most of all when he insists that language is other for *us all*, no matter how inconspicuously it operates in our lives.

But let us return now to the central claim of linguistic determinism, namely, that language is something that determines the way we think, making it impossible to think outside of the worldview it provides. Recall that this linguistic worldview is something that we share with others, but only those others with whom we share a language. Having now explored the descriptions that Heidegger and Derrida offer of language inheritance, we can now make clear what such a claim overlooks. First, we have come to see that being thrown into a discursive world does not mean that all possible meanings are worked out in advance. On the contrary, Dasein is continually "in the throw" of language. As Heidegger puts it in *On the Way to Language*, "There is no such thing as a natural language that would be the language of a human nature occurring of itself, without a destiny. All language is historical [*geschichtlich*]." [40] I have argued that this is precisely what the breakdown of everyday speech discloses—the continual throw, the need for reiteration, and thus the ever-present possibility of discourse's instability.

Next, linguistic determinism would seem to overlook what political power conceals—namely, that an ongoing reiteration of certain social arrangements underlies the relative stability of language conventions. If, however, language is ready-to-hand for us, even "determining" for us, its readiness-to-hand is often the result of how it is reiterated through the organization of our social world. On the one hand, this oversight is understandable. Because we are thrown into a world where language is already at work, for example, as part of our social rituals, it is easy to forget what makes language's power possible in the first place, that is, how it "works" in our lives. We relate to language for the most part pre-reflectively, and so this absorption is, to some degree, inevitable. Yet, as we have seen, even for a phenomenologist like Heidegger who takes seriously the pre-reflective character of our being-in-the-world, it is nevertheless crucial that we develop a more reflective relationship to the discourses we inherit. This reflective relationship is important for Heidegger, as it provides a more authentic way of inheriting the traditions in which we find ourselves. For later Continental philosophers like Derrida, though, it is important for another reason. It allows us to recognize and critically examine the history of the interpretive traditions we find ourselves in so that we can, where appropriate, revise or even radically transform these traditions.

Lastly, we can now see that linguistic determinism fails to recognize the difference that the instability of language makes in the lived experience of people, all of whom will at some point in their lives experience this instability. Indeed, it has no way of even recognizing the interpretive disputes that arise within a linguistic community—for example, the political controversy that can arise over the names of cities and streets. Such controversies become invisible when we assume that to speak a given language is to have it as an epistemic worldview, since then there would be no basis for any disagreement with others who share our language. Likewise, the linguistic determinist has no way of recognizing the ambiguous relationship to a given discourse that an individual person can experience while trying to make sense of the world through that discourse—an experience that, as we have seen, is actually quite common to all those who, on account of some hegemonic power structure—be it coloniality or patriarchy—become alienated from language. On the other hand, Heidegger and Derrida clearly acknowledge that such conflicts over language inheritance do exist, both within linguistic communities and for individual language users. In acknowledging the existence of these conflicts, they recognize the centrality of language for human existence while challenging the assumption that language provides a static, unchanging worldview.

It should be clear from this, then, that it would be a mistake to see Continental philosophers as offering only a deterministic theory of language. While it is true that philosophers like Heidegger and Derrida take seriously the way that discourses pre-reflectively set forth the world for us, they also recognize that this constitutes but one moment in the larger process that I have called the living life of language. As philosophers, we can begin to bring this larger process into view by examining more closely those situations in which people experience their relationship to language as ambiguous, that is, situations in which they feel both bound to language as the means by which the world is disclosed to them but also alienated from it. This kind of alienation occurs when people are rendered silent in some way by the language they rely on to disclose the world. This happens, for example, when a person relies on the disclosive power of medical discourse in a way that encourages her to engage in self-silencing, as we saw in the previous chapter. It also happens, as we saw in an earlier chapter, when a person finds himself still speaking and still thinking about the world through the language used by one's captor or torturer. Finally, such alienation can also occur, as we have seen in this chapter, when the mechanisms of colonial power discourage speakers of a language from reflecting on its colonial history. In such situations, the human relationship to language is far more complicated than that of an epistemic subject to an epistemic worldview. This complexity has dissuaded many philosophers from taking seriously such cases. However, as we have seen here, Continental philosophers have consistently taken interest in such cases as ways to better understand the important role that language plays in our lives and the conditions that allow us, as linguistic beings, to thrive.

NOTES

1. See Miranda Fricker's *Epistemic Injustice: Power and the Ethics of Knowing* (Oxford: Oxford University Press, 2007).

2. "Linguistic determinism" is another term for the Sapir-Whorf hypothesis mentioned in earlier chapters. Sapir presents the concept clearly when he writes, "It is quite an illusion to imagine that one adjusts to reality essentially without the use of language and that language is merely an incidental means of solving specific problems of communication or reflection. The fact of the matter is that the 'real world' is to a large extent unconsciously built up on the language habits of the group. No two languages are ever sufficiently similar to be considered as representing the same social

reality." Edward Sapir, "The Status of Linguistics as a Science," in *Selected Writings in Language, Culture, and Personality*, ed. David G. Mandelbaum (Berkeley: University of California Press, 1949), 162.

3. Ludwig Wittgenstein, *Tractatus Logico-Philosophicus*, trans. C. K. Ogden (New York: Routledge, 2005), 149 (5.6).

4. Richard Rorty, *Contingency, Irony, and Solidarity* (Cambridge: The Press Syndicate of the University of Cambridge, 1989), 21.

5. Graff situates Derrida within the school of postmodern literary theory, which he argues reduces truth to a play of language, thus denying the possibility of discovering first principles and thus eroding the concept of error. Gerald Graff, *Literature Against Itself: Literary Ideas in Modern Society* (Chicago: University of Chicago Press, 1979), 62. See also John W. Murphy's argument that sociologists can benefit from studying a theorist like Derrida, who makes clear how knowledge is always "shaped by acts of linguistic signification" and hence "linguistically prescribed." John W. Murphy, "Making Sense of Postmodern Sociology," *British Journal of Sociology* 39, no. 4 (1988): 604. See also David Novitz's "The Rage of Deconstruction," in which he argues that Derrida's philosophy entails linguistic idealism because it suggests that language is never constrained by a nonlinguistic world. David Novitz, "The Rage of Deconstruction," *Monist* 69, no. 1 (1986): 39–55.

6. As Lafont puts it, Heidegger views language as "the final authority for judging intraworldly knowledge," one that is not open to revision based on any intraworldly experience. She notes the resemblance between this and Humboldt's claim that every language "places definite boundaries upon the spirits of those who speak it." Cristina Lafont, *Heidegger, Language, and World-Disclosure*, trans. Graham Harman (Cambridge: Cambridge University Press, 2000), 7.

7. Jürgen Habermas, *The Philosophical Discourse of Modernity*, trans. Frederick G. Lawrence (Cambridge, MA: MIT Press, 1987), 152–54.

8. Jacques Derrida, *Monolingualism of the Other; or the Prosthesis of Origin*, trans. Patrick Mensah (Palo Alto, CA: Stanford University Press, 1998), 23.

9. Martin Heidegger, *Being and Time*, trans. John Macquarrie and Edward Robinson (New York: Harper & Row, 1962), 196.

10. Lawrence J. Hatab, *Proto-Phenomenology and the Nature of Language: Dwelling in Speech, Volume 1* (London: Rowman & Littlefield International, 2017), 130.

11. Richard Rorty, "Philosophy as Science, Metaphor, Politics," in *Essays on Heidegger and Others* (Cambridge: Cambridge University Press, 1991), 16.

12. Rorty, *Contingency, Irony, and Solidarity*, 50.

13. As Catherine Botha explains, through *Destruktion* the past becomes something we no longer take for granted but something that comes to claim us in some new, unanticipated way. Catherine Botha, "From *Destruktion* to Deconstruction: A Response to Moran," *South African Journal of Philosophy* 27, no. 1 (2008), 52–68.

14. Heidegger, *Being and Time*, 44.

15. Ibid., 43.

16. Heidegger's later work continues to be guided by this idea of destruction as a way of relating to historical tradition. In his 1951–1952 lectures, *What Is Called Thinking?*, he describes his approach to reading texts from the history of philosophy in this way: "People still hold the view that what is handed down to us by tradition is what in reality lies behind us—while in fact it comes toward us because we are its captives and destined to it. . . . That self-deception about history prevents us from hearing the language of the thinkers. . . . Hearing it presupposes that we meet a certain requirement, and we do so only on rare occasions. We must acknowledge and respect it. To acknowledge and respect consists in letting every thinker's thought come to us as something in each case unique, never to be repeated, inexhaustible—and being shaken to the depths by what is unthought in his thought." Martin Heidegger, *What Is Called Thinking?*, trans. Fred D. Wieck and J. Glenn Gray (New York: HarperCollins, 2004), 76–77.

17. Martin Heidegger, *Zollikon Seminars: Protocols, Conversations, Letters,* trans. Franz Mayr (Evanston, IL: Northwestern University Press, 2001). See also Carolyn Culbertson, "Losing the Measure of Health: Phenomenological Reflections on the Role of *Technē* in Healthcare Today," in *Existential Medicine : Essays on Health and Illness,* ed. Kevin Aho (London: Rowman & Littlefield International, 2018), 179–90.

18. Heidegger, *Being and Time,* 105.

19. Ibid., 105.

20. Martin Heidegger, *On the Way to Language,* trans. Peter Hertz (New York: Harper & Row, 1971), 57.

21. Ibid., 58.

22. Ibid., 59.

23. Heidegger, *Being and Time,* 217.

24. Ibid., 174.

25. Derrida, *Monolingualism of the Other,* 2.

26. Ibid., 1.

27. Ibid., 5.

28. As a result, since the 1962 revolution, there have been several laws to make Algerian Arabic the only language used in schools, on street signs, and in government and politics—the enforcement of which has not been very successful largely because of the population's linguistic diversity.

29. Rey Chow, *Not Like a Native Speaker: On Languaging as a Postcolonial Experience* (New York: Columbia University Press, 2014), 23.

30. Derrida, *Monolingualism of the Other,* 63.

31. This assumption appears especially problematic when we consider that the majority of the world's population today speaks more than one language. This fact alone demands that we rethink the assumption that one's language provides one with his or her "worldview."

32. Geoffrey Bennington, "Double Tonguing: Derrida's Monolingualism," in *Tympanum 4* (2000), 8.

33. Derrida, *Monolingualism of the Other,* 29.

34. Jacques Derrida, "Language is Never Owned: An Interview," in *Sovereignties in Question: The Poetics of Paul Celan,* ed. Thomas Dutoit and Outi Pasanen (New York: Fordham University Press, 2005), 104.

35. Derrida makes this point another way in "Signature, Event, Context," when he asks, "Could a performative utterance succeed if its formulation did not repeat a 'coded' or iterable utterance, or in other words, if the formula I pronounce in order to open a meeting, launch a ship or a marriage were not identifiable as a 'citation'?" To understand the citational aspect of speech acts is to see how their illocutionary force hinges on an invocation of history. Jacques Derrida, "Signature, Event, Context," in *Limited, Inc.,* trans. Samuel Weber and Jeffrey Mehlman (Evanston, IL: Northwestern University Press, 1988), 18.

36. Derrida, *Monolingualism of the Other,* 23–24.

37. Derrida distinguishes between force and power. "Force" refers to the material actions, sometimes violent, that help establish political and cultural forms of power, while, as Michael Naas explains, "power—as opposed to force—is always a phantasm," eliding a performative fiction with its real effects. Michael Naas, *Derrida from Now On* (New York: Fordham University Press, 2008), 200.

38. David Prochaska, *Making Algeria French: Colonialism in Bône, 1870–1920* (Cambridge: Cambridge University Press, 2002), 213.

39. In *Epistemic Injustice,* Miranda Fricker elaborates on how epistemic injustice rarely occurs independent of economic and other material forms of inequality. She argues that it is the backing of the latter that often makes attempts to remedy epistemic injustice so difficult. Fricker speaks much more about the role of material forms of inequality in perpetuating epistemic injustice than Derrida does or than I do in this chapter. However, my analysis here helps flesh out Fricker's claim that material forms

of inequality are "backed up and imaginatively justified" by the unequal distribution of hermeneutic authority. Fricker, *Epistemic Injustice*, 16.

40. Heidegger, *On the Way to Language*, 132.

Bibliography

Agamben, Giorgio. *Infancy and History: On the Destruction of Experience.* Translated by Liz Heron. London: Verso, 1993.
———. *Language and Death: The Place of Negativity.* Translated by Karen Pinkus and Michael Hardt. Minneapolis: University of Minnesota Press, 1991.
Aho, Kevin, and Charles Guignon. "Medicalized Psychiatry and the Talking Cure: A Hermeneutic Intervention." *Human Studies* 34, no. 3 (2011): 293–308.
Ake, Stacey E. "The Mystery Category 'Fourthness' and Its Relationship to the Work of C. S. Peirce." In *Walker Percy, Philosopher,* edited by Leslie Marsh, 63–88. London: Palgrave Macmillan, 2018.
Aler, Jan. "Heidegger's Conception of Language." In *On Heidegger and Language,* edited by Joseph J. Kockelmans, 33–62. Evanston, IL: Northwestern University Press, 1972.
Alfers, Sandra. "Poetry from the Theresienstadt Transit Camp, 1941–1945." *Rocky Mountain Review* 64, no. 1 (2010): 47–70.
American Psychiatric Association. *Diagnostic and Statistical Manual of Mental Disorders, Fifth Edition (DSM-V).* Arlington, VA: American Psychiatric Publishing, 2013.
Ardener, Edwin. "Belief and the Problem of Women." In *Perceiving Women,* edited by Shirley Ardener, 1–17. London: Malaby Press, 1975.
———. "The 'Problem' Revisited." In *Perceiving Women,* edited by Shirley Ardener, 19–27. London: Malaby Press, 1975.
Ardener, Shirley. *Defining Females: The Nature of Women in Society.* London: Croom Helm, 1978.
Arendt, Hannah. *The Human Condition.* Chicago: University of Chicago Press, 1998.
Aries, Elizabeth. *Men and Women in Interaction: Reconsidering the Differences.* Oxford: Oxford University Press, 1996.
Aristotle. *The Basic Works of Aristotle.* Edited by Richard McKeon. New York: Modern Library, 2001.
Austin, J. L. *How To Do Things with Words.* Cambridge, MA: Harvard University Press, 1975.
Bakhtin, Mikhail. *The Dialogic Imagination: Four Essays.* Edited by Michael Holquist. Translated by Caryl Emerson and Michael Holquist. Austin: University of Texas Press, 1981.
Barthes, Roland. *The Rustle of Language.* Translated by Richard Howard. Berkeley: University of California Press, 1989.
———. *Writing Degree Zero.* Translated by Annette Lavers and Colin Smith. New York: Hill & Wang, 1968.
Bartky, Sandra. *Femininity and Domination: Studies in the Phenomenology of Oppression.* New York: Routledge, 1990.
Beardsworth, Sara. *Julia Kristeva: Psychoanalysis and Modernity.* Albany: State University of New York Press, 2004.
Benhabib, Seyla. "Feminism and Postmodernism." In *Feminist Contentions: A Philosophical Exchange,* 17–34. New York: Routledge, 1995.
Bennington, Geoffrey. "Double Tonguing: Derrida's Monolingualism." *Tympanum* 4 (2000): 1–12.
Bernard, Jessie. "Talk, Conversation, Listening, Silence." In *The Sex Game: Communication between the Sexes,* 135–64. New York: Atheneum, 1972.

Bernasconi, Robert. *The Question of Language in Heidegger's History of Being.* Atlantic Highlands, NJ: Humanities International, 1985.

Bigger, Charles P. "Logos and Epiphany: Walker Percy's Theology of Language." In *Critical Essays on Walker Percy,* edited by J. Donald Crowley and Sue Mitchell Crowley, 49–57. Boston: G. K. Hall and Company, 1989.

Bindley, Katherine. "Women and Prescription Drugs: One in Four Takes Mental Health Drugs." *Huffington Post,* November 16, 2011. https://www.huffingtonpost.com/2011/11/16/women-and-prescription-drug-use_n_1098023.html.

Blanchot, Maurice. *The Infinite Conversation.* Translated by Susan Hanson. Minneapolis: University of Minnesota Press, 1993.

———. *The Space of Literature.* Translated by Ann Smock. Lincoln: University of Nebraska Press, 1982.

———. *The Writing of the Disaster.* Translated by Ann Smock. Lincoln: University of Nebraska, 1995.

Blanchot, Maurice, and Jacques Derrida. *The Instant of My Death / Demeure: Fiction and Testimony.* Translated by Elizabeth Rottenberg. Palo Alto, CA: Stanford University Press, 2008.

Blum, Linda M., and Nena F. Stracuzzi. "Gender and the Prozac Nation: Popular Discourse and Productive Femininity." *Gender and Society* 18, no. 3 (2004): 269–86.

Botha, Catherine. "From *Destruktion* to Deconstruction: A Response to Moran." *South African Journal of Philosophy* 27, no. 1 (2008): 52–68.

Brison, Susan. *Aftermath: Violence and the Remaking of a Self.* Princeton, NJ: Princeton University Press, 2003.

Brown, Laura S. "Empowering Depressed Women: The Importance of a Feminist Lens." In *Silencing the Self Across Cultures: Depression and Gender in the Social World,* edited by Dana Crowley Jack and Alisha Ali, 333–42. Oxford: Oxford University Press, 2010.

Bruns, Gerald L. *Modern Poetry and the Idea of Language.* New Haven, CT: Yale University Press, 1974.

Butler, Judith. *Gender Trouble : Feminism and the Subversion of Identity.* New York: Routledge, 1999.

———. *Giving an Account of Oneself.* New York: Fordham University Press, 2005.

———. "Imitation and Gender Insubordination." In *Inside Out: Lesbian Theories, Gay Theories,* edited by Diana Fuss, 13–31. New York: Routledge, 1991.

———. *Parting Ways: Jewishness and the Critique of Zionism.* New York: Columbia University Press, 2012.

———. *Undoing Gender.* New York: Routledge, 2004.

———. "What Is Critique?: An Essay on Foucault's Virtue." In *The Political: Readings in Continental Philosophy,* edited by David Ingram, 212–28. London: Blackwell, 2002.

Caldwell, David. "Reflections on holocaust and Holocaust." *Rocky Mountain Review* 64, no. 1 (2010): 11–16.

Cameron, Deborah. *Feminism and Linguistic Theory.* London: Macmillan, 1992.

Casey, Maud. "A Better Place to Live." In *Out of Her Mind: Women Writing on Madness,* edited by Rebecca Shannonhouse, 176–87. New York: Modern Library, 2003.

Celan, Paul. *Selected Poems and Prose of Paul Celan.* Translated by John Felstiner. New York: W. W. Norton, 2001.

Chodorow, Nancy. *The Reproduction of Mothering: Psychoanalysis and the Sociology of Gender.* Berkeley: University of California Press, 1978.

Chomsky, Noam. *Reflections on Language.* New York: Temple Smith, 1976.

Chow, Rey. *Not Like a Native Speaker: On Languaging as a Postcolonial Experience.* New York: Columbia University Press, 2014.

Cixous, Hélène. "The Laugh of Medusa." In *The Women and Language Debate: A Sourcebook,* edited by Camille Roman, Suzanne Juhasz, and Cristanne Miller, 78–93. New Brunswick, NJ: Rutgers University Press, 1994.

Coates, Jennifer. "Gossip Revisited: Language in All-Female Groups." In *Language and Gender: A Reader*, edited by Jennifer Coates and Pia Pichler, 199–223. Malden, MA: Wiley-Blackwell, 2011.

Code, Lorraine, ed. *Feminist Interpretations of Hans-Georg Gadamer*. University Park: Pennsylvania State University Press, 2003.

Coltman, Rod. *The Language of Hermeneutics: Gadamer and Heidegger in Dialogue*. Albany: State University of New York Press, 1998.

Cortina, Lilia M., and Vicki J. Magley. "Raising Voice, Risking Retaliation: Events Following Interpersonal Mistreatment in the Workplace." *Journal of Occupational Health Psychology* 8, no. 4 (2003): 247–65.

Crowley, Sue Mitchell. "Walker Percy's Wager: The Second Coming." In *Critical Essays on Walker Percy*, edited by J. Donald Crowley and Sue Mitchell Crowley, 225–42. Boston: G. K. Hall and Company, 1989.

Culbertson, Carolyn. "The Ethics of Relationality: Judith Butler and Social Critique." *Continental Philosophy Review* 46, no. 3 (2013): 449–63.

———. "Losing the Measure of Health: Phenomenological Reflections on the Role of *Technē* in Health Care Today." In *Existential Medicine: Essays on Health and Illness*, edited by Kevin Aho, 179–90. London: Rowman & Littlefield International, 2018.

Daly, Mary. *Gyn/Ecology: The Metaethics of Radical Feminism*. Boston: Beacon Press, 1978.

Derrida, Jacques. *Limited, Inc.* Translated by Samuel Weber and Jeffrey Mehlman. Evanston, IL: Northwestern University Press, 1988.

———. *Monolingualism of the Other; or the Prosthesis of Origin*. Translated by Patrick Mensah. Palo Alto, CA: Stanford University Press, 1998.

———. *Of Grammatology*. Translated by Gayatri Chakravorty Spivak. Baltimore: Johns Hopkins University Press, 1997.

———. *Sovereignties in Question: The Poetics of Paul Celan*. Edited by Thomas Dutoit and Outi Pasanen. New York: Fordham University Press, 2005.

———. *Speech and Phenomena*. Translated by David Allison. Evanston, IL: Northwestern University Press, 1973.

———. "Three Questions for Gadamer." In *Dialogue and Deconstruction: The Gadamer-Derrida Encounter*, edited by Diane P. Michelfelder and Richard E. Palmer, 52–54. Albany: State University of New York Press, 1989.

Dewey, Bradley R. "Walker Percy Talks about Kierkegaard: An Annotated Interview." *Journal of Religion* 54, no. 3 (July 1974): 273–98.

Dreyfus, Hubert L. *Being-in-the-World: A Commentary on Heidegger's Being and Time, Division I*. Cambridge, MA: MIT Press, 1992.

Emerson, Ralph Waldo. *Emerson: Essays and Poems*. New York: Library of America, 1996.

Emmons, Kimberly K. *Black Dogs and Blue Words: Depression and Gender in the Age of Self-Care*. New Brunswick, NJ: Rutgers University Press, 2010.

Engelland, Chad. *Ostension: Word Learning and the Embodied Mind*. Cambridge, MA: MIT Press, 2014.

Feldman, Karen S. *Binding Words: Conscience and Rhetoric in Hobbes, Hegel, and Heidegger*. Evanston, IL: Northwestern University Press, 2006.

Ferguson, Ann. *Blood at the Root: Motherhood, Sexuality, and Male Dominance*. London: Pandora, 1989.

Ferguson, Michaele L. "Sharing Without Knowing: Collective Identity in Feminist and Democratic Theory." *Hypatia* 22, no. 4 (2007): 30–45.

Foti, Veronique. *Heidegger and the Poets*. Atlantic Highlands, NJ: Humanities Press, 1992.

Foucault, Michel. *The History of Sexuality, Volume 1*. Translated by Robert Hurley. New York: Random House, 1978.

———. *Madness and Civilization: A History of Insanity in the Age of Reason*. Translated by Richard Howard. New York: Random House, 1965.

Frazer, Elizabeth, and Kimberly Hutchings. "Avowing Violence: Foucault and Derrida on Politics, Discourse, and Meaning." *Philosophy and Social Criticism* 37, no. 1 (2011): 3–23.

Freud, Sigmund. "Beyond the Pleasure Principle." In *The Freud Reader*, edited by Peter Gay. New York: W. W. Norton, 1989.

———. "Mourning and Melancholia." In *The Standard Edition of the Complete Psychological Works of Sigmund Freud*, 243–58. London: Hogarth, 1975.

Fricker, Miranda. *Epistemic Injustice: Power and the Ethics of Knowing*. Oxford: Oxford University Press, 2007.

Gadamer, Hans-Georg. "The Boundaries of Language." In *Language and Linguisticality in Gadamer's Hermeneutics*, translated and edited by Lawrence K. Schmidt, 9–18. Lanham, MD: Lexington, 2000.

———. *Gadamer on Celan: "Who Am I and Who Are You?" and Other Essays*. Translated and edited by Richard Heinemann and Bruce Krajewski. Albany: State University of New York Press, 1997.

———. *Philosophical Hermeneutics*. Translated and edited by David E. Linge. Berkeley: University of California Press, 1977.

———. *Truth and Method*. Translated by Joel Weinsheimer and Donald G. Marshall. London: Bloomsbury, 2004.

Gilligan, Carol. *In a Different Voice: Psychological Theory and Women's Development*. Cambridge, MA: Harvard University Press, 1982.

Gordon, Richard A. "Drugs Don't Talk: Do Medication and Biological Psychiatry Contribute to Silencing the Self?" In *Silencing the Self Across Cultures: Depression and Gender in the Social World*, edited by Dana Crowley Jack and Alisha Ali, 47–72. Oxford: Oxford University Press, 2010.

Graff, Gerald. *Literature Against Itself: Literary Ideas in Modern Society*. Chicago: University of Chicago Press, 1979.

Grassi, Ernesto. *Rhetoric as Philosophy: The Humanist Tradition*. University Park: Pennsylvania State University Press, 1980.

———. "Why Rhetoric Is Philosophy." *Philosophy and Rhetoric* 20, no. 2 (1987): 68–78.

Gross, Daniel M., and Ansgar Kemmann, eds. *Heidegger and Rhetoric*. Albany: State University of New York Press, 2005.

Habermas, Jürgen. "Leveling the Genre Distinction." In *The Derrida-Habermas Reader*. Chicago: University of Chicago Press, 2006.

———. *The Philosophical Discourse of Modernity*. Translated by Frederick G. Lawrence. Cambridge, MA: MIT Press, 1987.

———. *The Theory of Communicative Action, Volume 1: Reason and the Rationalization of Society*. Translated by Thomas McCarthy. Boston: Beacon Press, 1984.

———. *The Theory of Communicative Action, Volume 2: Lifeworld and System: A Critique of Functionalist Reason*. Translated by Thomas McCarthy. Boston: Beacon Press, 1984.

Hall, Judith A., Julie T. Irish, Debra L. Roter, Carol M. Ehrlich, and Lucy H. Miller. "Gender in Medical Encounters: An Analysis of Physician and Patient Communication in a Primary Care Setting." *Health Psychology* 13, no. 5 (1994): 384–92.

Hatab, Lawrence J. *Proto-Phenomenology and the Nature of Language: Dwelling in Speech, Volume 1*. London: Rowman & Littlefield International, 2017.

Hegel, G. W. F. *Phenomenology of Spirit*. Translated by A. V. Miller. Oxford: Oxford University Press, 1977.

Heidegger, Martin. *Basic Writings*. Edited by David Farrell Krell. New York: HarperCollins, 1993.

———. *Being and Time*. Translated by John Macquarrie and Edward Robinson. New York: Harper & Row, 1962.

———. *Hölderlin's Hymn: The Ister*. Translated by William McNeill and Julia Davis. Bloomington: Indiana University Press, 1966.

———. *Logic as the Question Concerning the Essence of Language*. Translated by Wanda Torres Gregory and Yvonne Unna. Albany: State University of New York Press, 2009.

————. *On the Essence of Language: The Metaphysics of Language and the Essencing of the Word*. Translated by Wanda Torres Gregory and Yvonne Unna. Albany: State University of New York Press, 2004.

————. *On the Way to Language*. Translated by Peter Hertz. New York: Harper & Row, 1971.

————. *Poetry, Language, Thought*. Translated by Albert Hofstadter. New York: HarperCollins, 2001.

————. *What Is Called Thinking?* Translated by Fred D. Wieck and J. Glenn Gray. New York: HarperCollins, 2004.

————. *Zollikon Seminars: Conversations, Protocols, Letters*. Translated by Franz Mayr. Evanston, IL: Northwestern University Press, 2001.

Heidegger, Martin, Hoseki Shin'ichi Hisamatsu, Alfred L. Copley, Hermann Gundert, Egon Vietta, Max Müller, and Landrat A. D. Siegfried Bröse. "Art and Thinking: Protocol of a Colloquium on May 18, 1958." Translated by Carolyn Culbertson and Tobias Keiling. *Philosophy Today* 61, no. 1 (2017): 47–51.

Hentrup, Miles. "Self-Completing Skepticism: On Hegel's Sublation of Pyrrhonism." *Epoché: A Journal for the History of Philosophy* 23, no. 1 (2018): 105–23.

Horwitz, Allan V., and Jerome C. Wakefield. *The Loss of Sadness: How Psychiatry Transformed Normal Sorrow into Depressive Disorder*. Oxford: Oxford University Press, 2007.

Howe, Irving. "Writing and the Holocaust." In *A Voice Still Heard: Selected Essays of Irving Howe*, edited by Nina Howe, 277–98. New Haven, CT: Yale University Press, 2014.

Husserl, Edmund. *The Crisis of the European Sciences and Transcendental Phenomenology: An Introduction to Phenomenological Philosophy*. Translated by David Carr. Evanston, IL: Northwestern University Press, 1970.

————. *Ideas: General Introduction to Pure Phenomenology*. Translated by W. R. Boyce Gibson. New York: Collier-Macmillan, 1962.

————. *Logical Investigations, Volume 2*. Edited by Dermot Moran. London: Routledge, 2001.

Inkpin, Andrew. *Disclosing the World: On the Phenomenology of Language*. Cambridge, MA: MIT Press, 2016.

Irigaray, Luce. "The Language of Man." Translated by Erin G. Carlston. *Cultural Critique* 13 (1989): 191–202.

————. *The Way of Love*. Translated by Heidi Bostic and Stephen Pluháček. London: Continuum, 2003.

Jack, Dana Crowley. *Silencing the Self: Women and Depression*. Cambridge, MA: Harvard University Press, 1991.

Jack, Dana Crowley, and Alisha Ali. "Introduction: Culture, Self-Silencing, and Depression: A Contextual-Relational Perspective." In *Silencing the Self Across Cultures: Depression and Gender in the Social World*, edited by Dana Crowley Jack and Alisha Ali, 3–18. Oxford: Oxford University Press, 2010.

Jakobson, Roman. "Shifters, Verbal Categories, and the Russian Verb." In *Word and Language, Volume 2 of Selected Writings*, 130–47. The Hague: Mouton, 1971.

Karp, David A. *Speaking of Sadness: Depression, Disconnection, and the Meanings of Illness*. Oxford: Oxford University Press, 1996.

Keller, Helen. *Helen Keller: Selected Writings*. Edited by Kim E. Nielsen. New York: New York University Press, 2005.

————. *Out of the Dark*. London: Hodder and Stoughton, 1913.

Kofman, Sarah. *Smothered Words*. Translated by Madeline Dobie. Evanston, IL: Northwestern University Press, 1998.

Kraepelin, Emil. "From 'Manic-Depressive Insanity' in Textbook Psychiatry, 8th edition, 1909–1915." In *The Nature of Melancholy: From Aristotle to Kristeva*, edited by Jennifer Radden, 259–80. Oxford: Oxford University Press, 2000.

Kramarae, Cheris. *Women and Men Speaking*. Rowley, MA: Newbury House, 1981.

Kristeva, Julia. *Black Sun: Depression and Melancholia*. Translated by Leon S. Roudiez. New York: Columbia University Press, 1989.

———. *Intimate Revolt: The Powers and Limits of Psychoanalysis*. Translated by Jeanine Herman. New York: Columbia University Press, 2002.

———. *Revolution in Poetic Language*. Translated by Margaret Waller. Introduction by Leon S. Roudiez. New York: Columbia University Press, 1984.

———. *The Sense and Non-sense of Revolt*. Translated by Jeanine Herman. New York: Columbia University Press. 1996.

———. *Tales of Love*. Translated by Leon S. Roudiez. New York: Columbia University Press, 1987.

———. *This Incredible Need to Believe*. Translated by Beverly Bie Brahic. New York: Columbia University Press, 2009.

Kristeva, Julia, and Dominique Grisoni. "Melancholia and Creation: An Interview with Dominique Grisoni." In *Julia Kristeva Interviews*, edited by Ross Mitchell Guberman, 78–84. New York: Columbia University Press, 1996.

Lacan, Jacques. *Écrits*. Translated by Bruce Fink. New York: W. W. Norton, 2006.

Lacoue-Labarthe, Phillipe. *Poetry as Experience*. Translated by Andrea Tarnowski. Palo Alto, CA: Stanford University Press, 1999.

Lafont, Cristina. *Heidegger, Language, and World-Disclosure*. Translated by Graham Harman. Cambridge: Cambridge University Press, 2000.

Lakoff, Robin. "Language and Women's Place." In *The Women and Language Debate: A Sourcebook*, edited by Camille Roman, Susan Juhasz, and Cristianne Miller, 280–91. New Brunswick, NJ: Rutgers University Press, 1994.

Lauder, Robert E. *Walker Percy: Prophetic, Existentialist, Catholic Storyteller*. New York: Lang, 1996.

Lawry, Edward G. "Literature as Philosophy." *Monist* 53 (1980): 547–57.

Lawson, Lewis A. "The Fall of the House of Lamar." In *The Art of Walker Percy: Stratagems for Being*, edited by Panthea Reid Broughton, 219–44. Baton Rouge: Louisiana State University Press, 1979.

Lechte, John. "Kristeva's *Soleil Noir* and Postmodernity." *Cultural Critique* 18, no. 18 (1991): 97–121.

Levi, Primo. *The Drowned and the Saved*. New York: Simon & Schuster, 1986.

Levinas, Emmanuel. *Totality and Infinity: An Essay on Exteriority*. Translated by Alphonso Lingis. Pittsburgh, PA: Duquesne University Press, 1969.

Longino, Helen. *The Fate of Knowledge*. Princeton, NJ: Princeton University Press, 2002.

———. *Science as Social Knowledge: Values and Objectivity in Scientific Inquiry*. Princeton, NJ: Princeton University Press, 1990.

Loy, David. *The World Is Made of Stories*. Somerville, MA: Wisdom Publications, 2010.

Lushchei, Martin. *The Sovereign Wayfarer: Walker Percy's Diagnosis of the Malaise*. Baton Rouge: Louisiana State University Press, 1972.

Lyon, James K. *Paul Celan and Martin Heidegger: An Unresolved Conversation, 1951–1970*. Baltimore: Johns Hopkins University Press, 2006.

Lyotard, Jean François. *The Differend: Phrases in Dispute*. Translated by Georges Van Den Abbeele. Minneapolis: University of Minnesota Press, 1988.

Lysaker, John. *You Must Change Your Life: Poetry, Philosophy, and the Birth of Sense*. University Park: Pennsylvania University Press, 2002.

Marx, Karl. *Capital: A Critique of Political Economy, Volume 1*. New York: International Publishers, 1967.

———. *Economic and Philosophical Manuscripts of 1844*. Translated by Martin Milligan. Amherst, NY: Prometheus Books, 1988.

Mattix, Micah. "Walker Percy's Alternative to Reductive Scientism in *The Thanatos Syndrome*." *Perspectives on Political Science* 40, no. 3 (2011): 147–52.

May, Reinhard. "Tezuka Tomio, An Hour with Heidegger." In *Heidegger's Hidden Sources: East Asian Influences on His Work*, translated by Graham Parkes, 59–64. London: Routledge, 1996.

Mazure, Carolyn M., Gwendolyn P. Keita, and Mary C. Blehar. *Summit on Women and Depression: Proceedings and Recommendations.* Washington, DC: American Psychological Association, 2002.

McCumber, John. *The Company of Words: Hegel, Language, and Systematic Philosophy.* Evanston, IL: Northwestern University Press, 2003.

Merleau-Ponty, Maurice. *Phenomenology of Perception.* Translated by Colin Smith. London: Routledge, 2002.

Mills, Sara. "Discourse Competence: Or How to Theorize Strong Women Speakers." *Hypatia: A Journal of Feminist Philosophy* 7, no. 2 (1992): 4–17.

Moore, Benita A. "Language as Sacrament in Walker Percy's 'The Second Coming.'" *Journal of the American Academy of Religion* 60, no. 2 (1992): 281–99.

Moore, G. E. "A Defence of Common Sense." In *Contemporary British Philosophy*, edited by J. H. Muirhead, 192–233. London: George Allen & Unwin, 1925.

Murphy, John W. "Making Sense of Postmodern Sociology." *British Journal of Sociology* 39, no. 4 (1988): 600–614.

Naas, Michael. *Derrida from Now On.* New York: Fordham University Press, 2008.

Nietzsche, Friedrich. "On Truth and Lie in an Extra-Moral Sense." In *The Portable Nietzsche*, translated and edited by Walter Kaufmann, 42–47. New York: Penguin, 1982.

Nikolchina, Miglena. *Matricide in Language: Writing Theory in Kristeva and Woolf.* New York: Other Press, 2004.

Novalis. "Monologue." In *The German Library: German Romantic Criticism.* Translated by Alexander Gelley, edited by Ernst Behler. New York: Continuum, 1982.

Novitz, David. "The Rage of Deconstruction." *Monist* 69, no. 1 (1986): 39–55.

Oliver, Kelly. "The Crisis of Meaning." In *The Kristeva Critical Reader*, edited by John Lechte and Mary Zournazi, 36–54. Edinburgh: Edinburgh University Press, 2003.

———. *Subjectivity without Subjects: From Abject Fathers to Desiring Mothers.* Lanham, MD: Rowman & Littlefield, 1998.

Ong, Walter. *Orality and Literacy.* London: Routledge, 2012.

Palmer, Richard E. *Hermeneutics: Interpretation Theory in Schleiermacher, Dilthey, Heidegger, and Gadamer.* Evanston, IL: Northwestern University Press, 1969.

Pappas, Robin, and William Cowling. "Toward a Critical Hermeneutics." In *Feminist Interpretations of Hans-Georg Gadamer*, edited by Lorraine Code, 203–27. University Park: Pennsylvania State University Press, 2003.

Parkes, Graham. "Afterwords—Language." In *Heidegger and Asian Thought*, edited by Graham Parkes, 213–16. Honolulu: University of Hawaii Press, 1987.

Pateman, Carole. *The Sexual Contract.* Palo Alto, CA: Stanford University Press, 1988.

Percy, Walker. *The Message in the Bottle: How Queer Man Is, How Queer Language Is, and What One Has to Do with the Other.* New York: Picador, 1975.

———. *Signposts in a Strange Land.* New York: Picador, 1991.

Perkins, Karey. "Diamonds in the Rough: The Peirce-Percy Semiotic in *The Second Coming*." In *Walker Percy, Philosopher*, edited by Leslie Marsh, 89–114. London: Palgrave Macmillan, 2018.

Pinker, Steven. *The Stuff of Thought: Language as a Window into Human Nature.* New York: Penguin, 2007.

Plato. *Plato: Complete Works.* Edited by John M. Cooper. Indianapolis: Hackett, 1997.

Pöggeler, Otto. "Heidegger's Topology of Being." In *On Heidegger and Language*, edited by Joseph J. Kockelmans, 107–46. Evanston, IL: Northwestern University Press, 1972.

Prochaska, David. *Making Algeria French: Colonialism in Bône, 1870–1920.* Cambridge: Cambridge University Press, 2002.

Rich, Adrienne. *The Dream of a Common Language: Poems 1974–1977.* New York: W. W. Norton, 1978.

Riley, Denise. *The Words of Selves: Identification, Solidarity, Irony.* Palo Alto, CA: Stanford University Press, 2000.

Risser, James. *Hermeneutics and the Voice of the Other: Re-reading Gadamer's Philosophical Hermeneutics*. Albany: State University of New York Press, 1997.

Rizzolatti, Giacomo, and Corrado Sinigaglia. *Mirrors in the Brain: How Our Minds Share Actions and Emotions*. Oxford: Oxford University Press, 2008.

Rorty, Richard. *Contingency, Irony, and Solidarity*. Cambridge: The Press Syndicate of the University of Cambridge, 1989.

———. *Essays on Heidegger and Others*. Cambridge: Cambridge University Press, 1991.

———. *The Linguistic Turn: Essays in Philosophical Method*. Chicago: University of Chicago Press, 1967.

Ross, Stephen David. *The Limits of Language*. New York: Fordham University Press, 1994.

Ryle, Gilbert. "Heidegger's *Sein und Zeit*." In *Heidegger and Modern Philosophy*, edited by Michael Murray, 53–64. New Haven, CT: Yale University Press, 1978.

Sapir, Edward. *Selected Writings in Language, Culture, and Personality*. Edited by David G. Mandelbaum. Berkeley: University of California Press, 1949.

Scarry, Elaine. *The Body in Pain: The Making and Unmaking of the World*. Oxford: Oxford University Press, 1985.

Schleiermacher, Friedrich. *Hermeneutics and Criticism*. Cambridge: Cambridge University Press, 1998.

Schmidt, Dennis. *Lyrical and Ethical Subjects: Essays on the Periphery of the Word, Freedom, and History*. Albany: State University of New York Press, 2005.

Schmidt, Lawrence K. "Language in Hermeneutic Ontology." In *Language and Linguisticality in Gadamer's Hermeneutics*, edited by Lawrence K. Schmidt, 1–8. Lanham, MD: Lexington, 2000.

Schneider, Michael J., and Karen A. Foss. "Thought, Sex, and Language: The Sapir-Whorf Hypothesis in the American Women's Movement." *Women's Studies in Communication* 1, no. 1 (1977): 1–7.

Scott, Joan W. "Deconstructing Equality-Versus-Difference: Or, the Uses of Poststructuralist Theory for Feminism." In *Feminist Social Thought*, edited by Diana T. Meyers, 757–69. London: Routledge, 1997.

Scott, Kathryn. "Perceptions of Communication Competence: What's Good for the Goose is Not Good for the Gander." *Women's Studies International Quarterly* 3, no. 2 (1990): 199–208.

Sheehan, Thomas. *Making Sense of Heidegger: A Paradigm Shift*. London: Rowman & Littlefield, 2014.

Shenker, Noah. *Reframing Holocaust Testimony*. Bloomington: Indiana University Press, 2015.

Spender, Dale. *Man Made Language*. London: Routledge & Kegan Paul, 1980.

Stoppard, Janet. "Women's Bodies, Women's Lives and Depression: Towards a Reconciliation of Material and Discursive Accounts." In *Body Talk: The Material and Discursive Regulation of Sexuality, Madness, and Reproduction*, edited by Jane M. Ussher, 10–32. New York: Routledge, 1997.

Stoppard, Janet M., and Deanna J. Gammell. "Depressed Women's Treatment Experiences: Exploring Themes of Medicalization and Empowerment." In *Situating Sadness: Women and Depression in Social Context*, edited by Janet M. Stoppard and Linda M. McMullen, 39–61. New York: New York University Press, 2003.

Szondi, Peter. *Celan Studies*. Palo Alto, CA: Stanford University Press, 2003.

Taylor, Charles. *The Language Animal: The Full Shape of the Human Linguistic Capacity*. Cambridge, MA: The Belknap Press of Harvard University Press, 2016.

Ussher, Jane. *Women's Madness: Misogyny or Mental Illness*. Amherst: University of Massachusetts Press, 1992.

Utz, Stephen. "Percy, Peirce, and Parsifal: Intuition's Farther Shore." In *Walker Percy, Philosopher*, edited by Leslie Marsh, 21–40. London: Palgrave Macmillan, 2018.

Vallega, Alejandro A. *Sense and Finitude: Encounters at the Limits of Language, Art, and the Political*. Albany: State University of New York Press, 2009.

Warnke, Georgia. "Hermeneutics and Constructed Identities." In *Feminist Interpretations of Hans-Georg Gadamer*, edited by Lorraine Code, 57–80. University Park: Pennsylvania State University Press, 2003.

―――. "Race, Gender, and Antiessentialist Politics." *Signs: Journal of Women in Culture and Society* 31, no. 1 (2005): 93–116.

Watters, Ethan. *Crazy Like Us: The Globalization of the American Psyche*. New York: Free Press, 2010.

Whorf, Benjamin Lee. *Language, Thought, and Reality: Selected Writings of Benjamin Lee Whorf*. Cambridge, MA: MIT Press, 1956.

Wittgenstein, Ludwig. *Philosophical Investigations*. Translated by G. E. M. Ascombe. Oxford: Blackwell Publishing, 2001.

―――. *Tractatus Logico-Philosophicus*. Translated by C. K. Ogden. New York: Routledge, 2005.

Ziarek, Krzysztof. *Inflected Language: Toward a Hermeneutics of Nearness: Heidegger, Levinas, Stevens, Celan*. Albany: State University of New York Press, 1994.

Zoellner, Tanja, and Susanne Hedlund. "Women's Self-Silencing and Depression in the Socio-Cultural Context of Germany." In *Silencing the Self Across Cultures: Depression and Gender in the Social World*, edited by Dana Crowley Jack and Alisha Ali, 107–28. Oxford: Oxford University Press, 2010.

Zolkos, Magdalena. "*No Pasarán*: Trauma, Testimony, and Language for Paul Celan." *The European Legacy* 14, no. 3 (2009): 269–82.

Index

affectivity, 85, 94, 95, 96, 97, 97–98
Algeria, 114, 115, 116, 119, 120, 124n28
Ali, Alisha, 92
alienation, linguistic, 2–3, 3–4, 5, 5–6,
7–9, 46, 52–53, 55, 57, 59, 64, 67, 75,
78, 86, 87, 105–106, 107, 116–117,
118, 120, 121–122
Anglo-American Philosophy, 6, 15, 106
Antelme, Robert, 46, 50, 51, 52, 53, 54,
55, 59, 63
archaic preobject, 88, 89, 90, 91, 92,
96–97, 98
Arendt, Hannah, 14, 17
Aristotle, 13, 27n1
Austin, J. L., 103n41
authenticity, 113, 120; linguistic
authenticity, 73, 74, 79

backchannel communication, 77–78
Barthes, Roland, 48
Bartky, Sandra, 74–79, 84
being-in-the-world, 6, 22, 31, 108, 109,
121
Bennington, Geoffrey, 117
Blanchot, Maurice, 46–50, 50, 51, 54, 56,
57, 59, 60n7, 60n10
Brison, Susan, 53
Butler, Judith, 10, 46, 51, 67–71, 72,
73–74, 80n14, 80n18, 81n25, 81n26,
107, 110, 117

Celan, Paul, 8, 46, 51, 52, 54, 55–57, 58,
59, 61n23, 63
Chomsky, Noam, 15
Chow, Rey, 116
Cixous, Hélène, 67, 69, 70–71, 73
colonialism, 115–116, 117, 119, 119–120,
121–122
computer language, 9, 10, 18, 34

continental philosophy, 4–5, 5–7, 8–10,
10, 11, 15, 27, 29n23, 41, 46, 54, 59,
63–64, 67, 74, 86, 87, 105, 107, 109,
110, 111, 114, 121, 122
conversation, 8, 14, 18, 26, 39, 40, 41, 45,
57, 63, 66, 72, 74, 77–78, 85
critique, 10, 69, 71, 73, 74, 107, 120

Daly, Mary, 65, 69
Dasein, 22, 24, 26, 32, 33, 107, 108, 109,
113
deconstruction, 107
depression, 86, 91, 93, 94, 99, 100n1,
101n9, 103n36; biomedical model of,
83–84, 88, 101n10, 101n13; Julia
Kristeva's theory of, 87, 88, 89, 92,
94–96, 97, 98, 110; women and, 7, 79,
84, 85, 85–86, 88, 91, 93, 98, 100n5,
100n7, 101n14
Derrida, Jacques, 4, 8, 9, 42n19, 46, 48,
55–56, 56–59, 61n28, 61n30, 61n33,
63, 107, 111, 114–119, 120–122,
123n5, 124n35, 124n37, 124n39
Destruktion , 110, 114, 123n13, 123n16
determinism, linguistic, 65, 71, 80n5,
106–108, 109, 113, 116, 120–121,
122n2
diagnostic speech, 68, 83, 85–86, 87,
87–88, 91, 94, 97–99, 101n13, 110, 119
dialogue, 8, 10, 15, 39, 40, 95, 97

emotional caretaking, 75, 75–78, 93
epistemology, 3, 5, 9, 10, 106; epistemic
injustice, 106, 124n39; epistemic
worldview, 78, 106, 106–108, 109,
113, 114, 121–122
ethics, 4, 8, 58, 67, 71, 73, 76, 78
exploitation, 75, 78

About the Author

Carolyn Culbertson is associate professor of philosophy at Florida Gulf Coast University. She has published articles in journals including *Southwest Philosophy Review*, *IJFAB: International Journal of Feminist Approaches to Bioethics*, *Continental Philosophy Review*, *Philosophy Today*, and *Comparative and Continental Philosophy*. She is cofounder of the Southwest Florida Feminist Community Reading Group and vice president of the North American Society for Philosophical Hermeneutics.